"If it's not on the trolley, you can't have it."

by

Gary May

Bloomington, IN Milton Keynes, UK

AuthorHouse™
1663 Liberty Drive, Suite 200
Bloomington, IN 47403
www.authorhouse.com
Phone: 1-800-839-8640

AuthorHouse™ UK Ltd.
500 Avebury Boulevard
Central Milton Keynes, MK9 2BE
www.authorhouse.co.uk
Phone: 08001974150

This book is a work of non-fiction. Unless otherwise noted, the author and the publisher make no explicit guarantees as to the accuracy of the information contained in this book and in some cases, names of people and places have been altered to protect their privacy.

First published by AuthorHouse 5/31/2006

ISBN: 1-4259-3361-0 (sc)

Printed in the United States of America and the United Kingdom

This book is printed on acid-free paper.

ACKNOWLEDGMENTS

Originally this book started out as a kind of self
−counseling exercise to try and come to terms with my
airline life and understand how fate and destiny are
meant to happen.

After writing the book I approached a few good
friends of mine Simon Reeve, Jamie Davies, Douglas
Love, Debbie Bliss and Lyne Emerson, asking them
to read the manuscript and let me know their opinions
and feelings about it.

It was from their reactions that I realised I had
captured something on paper that was very real, very
readable and a bit special.

Throughout the writing process I would like to
thank Simon Reeve for assisting me in editing this
story and all the hysterical laughs we had going through
the various chapters over many cups of coffee. To
Lucy Golding who typed it all from the hand written

manuscript, Dougie Love, Jamie Davies, Debbie Bliss and Lynne Emerson for their continual reassurance that the book was fascinating, inspiring and should be published.

There are many who have helped me throughout my career particularly whilst flying and it would be remiss not to mention them .So many thanks to Malcolm McKinnon, Andy Reed ,Alex Chisnall , Phillo Beddo ,Simon Wood-Wooley,Chris Brogan ,Andy Club,Captain Tim Hiles and his wife Barbara, Rachel, Billy Penny , Justine Lake , Ozzie Waine , Jules Stenson from the News of the World and Chris Ginger Rowe for all the happy memories, good times and wonderful trips.

Thanks also to all my friends from Darlington Golf Club and Tenerife who always had comforting advice and encouragement, in particular Richie Bearpark, Neil Young, Trevor Mann, Peter Kelly ,Stuart Beveridge ,Steve Chapman , Tony Lancaster ,Arthur Ellis, Brian Hirst, Philly Dog Patterson ,Jez the Steward and Dave Elliott.

On the family front, special thanks to Mam and Dad who have always been there and helped me so much with endless patience, understanding, support and love.

This is for you.

Gary May

The inspiration for me to write this book came after spending 36 hours locked up in a Spanish jail on Tenerife.

What you are about to read is an intriguing insight into airline life. The characters I came across, the bullying and favouritism, fun and laughter, great trips, love and romance, heartache and sadness, it's a roller-coaster ride. So make sure you have the front seat for a story covering a ten year period. Fasten your seatbelts and enjoy the flight.

The story begins.......

1992   Mallorca,
working as a holiday rep.

I am sat outside the Resort Manager's office waiting to be called in. The previous night had been the end of summer-season party, and things had got a bit wild. Kelly Lennon, the Resort Manager had kept her camera on one of the tables. I took it on myself to borrow it for an hour and proceeded to take pictures of the male reps bums and penises in the toilets, including several of mine! I carefully replaced the camera back on Kelly's table without her noticing and carried on partying.

The following lunchtime I received a call at the hotel 'Don Bigote', Palma Nova where I was one of the holiday reps, Kelly wanted to see me and she was less than happy. I had been a holiday rep for about four years. In fact when I joined in 1988 I think we were called couriers and you had to know at least a bit of the local language. The money was good, (four times what they earn today) and it was quite a sought after job.

As I pondered my fate outside Kelly's office my mind wandered back over the four years of non-stop parties and good times, then the door opened.

"Come in Gary, take a seat" said Kelly.

She was a sullen-faced, hard-nosed dragon who had a permanent, miserable, fish-faced expression. I had been under her supervision for about two months, having moved from another resort because of an incident with a Spanish coach driver who had assaulted one of the reps sister's. I happened to step in and accidently belted him. It was decided I had better move resorts as it was all very political at that time in Mallorca.

"May I say I am totally disgusted, flabbergasted and humiliated" Kelly raged at me, "do you know where I've been today?" she went on.

"The V.D Clinic?" I asked apprehensively

"Not very funny, I have been to the photo-shop to get my pictures developed"

"Oh!" I replied.

"Oh is right, and this is what I was given". She produced a folder and spilled the pictures onto the table. "Twenty eight of men's penises and six of the party" she raged. Without drawing breath she continued, "When I went to collect them I wondered why the shop assistant was smiling so much, he must think I am a nymphomaniac or something, all these men's willies on one film". She sighed.

I was desperately trying to hold myself together. When you're drunk you do some strange things, but this was hysterical.

"Yeah so what's it got to do with me?" I responded.

"You're responsible for this, it's your doing! I know it! That's your penis, and I'm sure one of those belongs to Tommy Sex, your best mate" Kelly continued.

Behind a hidden smile, I denied all knowledge of the events. Then she dropped the bombshell that would strangely alter the course of my life, (and if it hadn't happened this book wouldn't have been written)

"Well I've decided to take away your winter work" she said.

Gulp, dry hands, nausea etc...

"Yes, I've been onto Head Office and it's been agreed. Gary, you are out of control, you're a very funny guy but you don't know where to draw the line. You need to have a six month break, you've belted a coach driver albeit he deserved it, you are rude to me; you've taken these pictures, (not proven) so it's time for a break. You will still have your job with David Elliot in Ibiza for the summer, but that's the decision".

That evening I walked back to my hotel in deep shock, I felt sick. It was mid October and the weather had cooled slightly after a hot, vibrant, crazy summer.

I was in shock, what the fuck was I going to do, all I knew was repping and partying, and I was excellent at both.

I crept into the hotel, sullen and down at heart. Tommy Sex, a fellow rep in the hotel was there to meet me. "Have you heard the news?" I said to him.

"Yes, those bastards can't do that. We will get a petition drawn up, strike etc!" he replied.

I was inconsolable, and slumped at my reps desk.

I had been working with Tommy Sex for a couple of months. He was a scouse nutter who was only doing the job for one thing, hence his nickname. I'm still good friends with him today. We had a lot of fun working together. There were two telephones on the desk, one worked the other didn't. If a holiday maker came up to ask about the weather we would pretend to phone Michael Fish at the BBC Weather Centre in London and the conversation would go as follows:

"Hello Michael. Gazza here in Mallorca, one of the reps. just wondering what the weather's going to be like today? Hmmm…! Eh right, great Michael, thanks"

We would then advise the guests that Michael Fish had said it was going to be 90 f and they would walk away happy. We would then all fall about laughing.

The telephone would come in particularly handy for guest's complaints, when we would pretend to phone up Head Office and give them an almighty bollocking for the standard of the accommodation. As the guests only stood about four feet away they were more than happy with our customer care procedure of getting things done.

That evening a couple of people came over to speak to me and I confided in them a little about what had happened over the last forty eight hours. They listened intently, laughed a lot and gave me some nice encouragement, (good person, funny, out-going, hilarious etc). On leaving the table, one of them handed me The Daily Express. As I aimlessly flicked through it, something stopped me in my tracks and would change my life forever.

"Job Advertisement. Virgin Airlines: Cabin-crew required".

Let me now take you on a most intriguing and fascinating journey.

CHAPTER 1

THE NEW BEGINNING

The application form had been sent off and the interview date set. In the meantime I had moved to Crawley near Gatwick Airport, into a rented house or should I say, a rented room in someone's house; Gail was the landlady.

I had started seeing a Caledonian cabin-crew girl called Corinne, a cracking brunette from Birmingham, and had also landed a job at Kuoni Travel doing sales and marketing. However my heart was set on flying, see the world for nothing and get someone else to pay for it. Long haul, none of this back and forward to Palma in a day. Proper trips and fantastic parties!

The interview went well, it started off with twenty people and eventually dwindled down to three, of which I was one, plus two other beautiful girls.

"Well Gary, we will let you know". Those were their finishing words and with a cheeky wink from one of them, I knew I had the job.

Two days later the letter dropped through the letter box at No.4, The Canter in Crawley, West Sussex. "Congratulations. Welcome to Virgin Atlantic, your salary will be £6900 plus flying allowance, your starting date is: 04 – 01 – 94".

"Yeah Ha:" I screamed. This was it! The chance to see the world and have a great time.

I hadn't told Corinne that I had applied for the job as she had a policy of not going out with airline crew because they couldn't stay faithful and previously, she had suffered a broken heart, a bad one.

Corinne had been on a trip to Mallorca the day the letter came so I hadn't had the chance to tell her and didn't know how she would react to the news. I informed Kuoni Travel that day of my intentions and they were brilliant, an excellent company, I had enjoyed working for them but it was time to move on.

Corinne came to my house that night and I anxiously brought up the subject of my new intended career; she was tired after her flight so I chose the moment carefully.

'Hey Corinne, I got a new job today" I said, very chuffed.

"Oh really" she replied. I think she thought I'd got a new promotion at Kuoni Travel.

"Yeah, flying long haul for Virgin Atlantic" I said nervously. Smack! Punch! She cracked me right across the face then screaming, ran out of the room in tears. (hmm! she's happy with that decision then).

I spent the next few days trying to reassure her that everything would be ok, that it was just a job like any other, but she was inconsolable. Her ex of major heartache happened to be ex – Virgin crew and she kept going on about the wild parties and exotic locations. I was trying hard to hide my excitement but it was tough.

Corinne decided to take some unpaid leave from her work to go and visit her sister in Australia while my training course was underway, and then see how she felt on her return.

I decided to call the lads at Darlington Golf Club and tell them of my pending career move. Hopefully they would give me a better reception. Darlington Golf Club is a unique place in golfing and social folk-law, it's a great place to visit and be involved.

Not only are there some amazing social characters and personalities, but it is also a place of sanctuary where you can go when times are hard or when you've had a bad experience like a death in the family or something similar.

My really close friends up North loved it when I was a holiday rep; it was free holidays for them wherever I was working including free drinks in all the bars and clubs as well as loads of great women to be introduced.

How would they take the news of my airline move? Answer – very badly!

It was Friday night and I knew all the boys would be up at the club having a few beers before going into town to get wasted.

Darlington Golf Club. North East England. I was phoning my mates: ring ring! ring ring!

"Hello, Darlington Golf Club' said the voice on the other end.

"Hi, can I speak to Steve Chapman please?" I asked.

"Sure, one minute" came the reply. The steward Barry called out for Steve to come to the phone. I could hear the usual buzz, banter and laughter in the background. I loved that place and wanted to be there, especially as it was Friday night.

"Who is it?" a voice called out in the background, the steward then asked me and I told him,

"It's Gazza".

The steward shouted out "It's Gazza!"

A big cheer went up and Steve came to the phone.

"Steve! How's things mate?" I asked.

"Excellent, we've just been talking about you and planning the summer holiday to Ibiza" he said.

I had to stop him in his tracks.

"The thing is Steve I'm not repping this year. I've had a career change" I replied.

"Oh yes and what you going to be doing?" he enquired.

I took a deep breath.

"Well, I've joined Virgin Airlines as cabin-crew" I blurted out as quickly as possible. A deathly silence fell over the phone. I repeated myself a couple of times and then Steve shouted out to everyone in the bar;

"Gazza is going to be an air-hostess!" A huge roar of laughter went up. I was dying on the other end of the phone. Then the banter started.

"Tea, coffee, if it's not on the trolley you can't have it." All the lads in the bar then started singing in unison.

"You're gay and you know you are, you're gay and you wear a wonder-bra." at fever pitch volume. I had to laugh. I would have done the same had I been there and if it had been one of the other lads in the same position. I tried to defend my corner, telling them that it was really fit girls I would be working with, that if all the blokes were gay, more women for me, but they weren't having it. Richie, one of the lads asked out loud,

"Does he have to wear stockings?" More laughter!

"Well, that's really inconsiderate of you. What about our usual holiday?" Steve said.

"At this point in my life I've got to think about my future" I replied, but it fell on deaf ears.

I am lucky to possess the greatest parents in the world. They are totally brilliant and have always

5

been110% supportive on whatever I decided to do in life. A lot of people think we are not related because I'm so wild and they are so quiet and reserved, Mum thinks she picked up the wrong baby at the hospital.

I've put them through some traumatic situations over the years, but they have always been there for me. Mum is a little bit scared of flying, I always tell her it's not the flying she should be scared about, its' the crashing.

Over the phone I explained my reasons for taking this career move and they agreed I should go for it.

When I had been repping, Mum and Dad would visit me and come on all the wild trips, bar crawls, cruises and beach parties. I remember on one occasion when there were fifty drunks on my coach going wild whilst driving through Palma in Mallorca, Dad and I were throwing straw donkeys out of the bus window. It was great fun then but now, they could come to New York, Miami, Japan and all the rest of the world.

The training date was 04 – 01 – 94, and I had to pass the course yet.

I spent Christmas at home and the New Year down at Crawley. I was so looking forward to getting started, it couldn't come quick enough. The night before the training began I spent looking through the pre-course booklet they had sent out, destinations we flew to, New York JFK, Boston, Newark, New Jersey, Los Angeles, Orlando, Miami, Narita Japan and Moscow; my mind started to wander, all these mouth-watering, fantastic places, Wow! This was going to be great!

The cabin-crew job didn't worry me at all, doing the safety demo and serving people didn't bother me either. My only concern was going around the plane with a teapot in my hand. This troubled me greatly, as no matter how hard you tried walking down the aisle saying, 'anyone for tea' trying to look manly or butch, it was a physical impossibility, even Arnold Schwarzenegger couldn't do it, you just look and sound so gay.

CHAPTER 2

DAY ONE, "TRAINING".

I was a little late arriving at the training course venue; it was being held in a small office complex on a Crawley industrial estate, not like the grand offices the company possesses today. At the time I joined Virgin Airlines it was going through a big expansion programme.

As I made my way to the make-shift classroom, I held my breath on approaching the door. In I wandered only to be greeted by the most amazing sight; fourteen beautiful, sexy, young women and one other bloke, (he must be gay I thought). The training course would be six weeks long in order to cover all aspects of flying. Happy days I thought. I have made the right decision!

Group 94 Training course

Six weeks of intense training followed: The first morning we all made our introductions, basically each of the girls was previously either a model or had done similar promotional work. They were all beautiful and had lovely personalities as well.

About 30% of them would leave within 3 months due to jealous boyfriends, or the job just wasn't for them. The other guy on the course George (or Muskrat as he would become known) , was a rugby player from Wales and quite obviously not gay .He must have signed up for the same reasons as myself; we would become lifelong friends and experience lots of mad things together

The first two weeks of the training course were quite hard going, a lot to take in, plenty of homework and studying every night.

The two instructors were great though, and made things more bearable. Janice was a Meg Ryan look-alike and had a great sense of fun, the other girl Karen was 6 months pregnant but was well chilled-out and had been flying for years.

We would watch videos of air-crashes, (Kegworth and unseen footage of Lockerbie etc), quite harrowing some of it. Aircraft visits were organised for all of us to look over the Jumbo 747and discover its inner workings. Each morning a test would take place to see if you had absorbed the information from the previous day. I had never experienced so many early nights but I knew it would be worth it.

At the end of the third week I decided to let my hair down and have a good Friday night out. The venue would be The Parsons Pig pub, just outside Crawley. The place was run by Don and his good wife together with six or seven good fun bar staff. In the early nineties, before the area became properly developed and the big Corporate Companies moved in, this pub and the Six Bells in Horley were the hot spots of the day.

In Crawley, at that time, all the major airlines had thousands of employees living there, mostly renting. People would come because it was next to Gatwick airport and make the town their base and home for the coming season.

Since airline work was mainly shifts every night of the week, during that time, was like a Saturday night. All the crews from Virgin, British Airways, Britannia, Monarch, and Scandic Air etc would descend on The Parsons Pig. It was a vibrant pub with a brilliant atmosphere, full of light-hearted young people, and a great place to party. Pulling was common and very easy to do.

A group of us headed down there to let our hair down, including Muskrat, a couple of girls from my training course, Philo Beddo a golfing friend of mine and Timmy "Cheque Book" who lived in the same house where I rented. Timmy had earned his nickname because he never carried cash. On one occasion he was playing golf and as his ball was on the green, he rummaged in his pocket for a coin to mark it. He couldn't find one, so he pulled out his folded cheque book and used that instead (the name has stuck ever since).

Gay Guy from Monarch Air also came along - he had been a holiday rep with me the previous summer but left to join the airline. During his six months as cabin-crew he had become exceptionally camp and I wasn't sure which team he was batting for anymore. Amazing, as he was a top shagger in Mallorca!

We had a great night and I managed to pull a cracking Scottish girl, Julie, from Monarch. In a drunken state we staggered back to my house for mad sex; she didn't disappoint! The following morning, in a haze and feeling exceptionally rough, I opened my eyes and stared at the clock – 12.05. Julie was fast asleep beside me and I needed a drink big time. At the bottom of the bed was a straw sombrero that I had acquired from the previous nights partying. I popped it on my head and promptly thundered down the stairs to the fridge, I was totally naked apart from my hat and a semi-erect penis. After acquiring a bottle of water, for some mad reason I then decided to do a kind of semi-jig / Highland-fling dance and skipped into the living room.

As I bounded in I was stopped dead in my tracks by the vision in front of me.

"My God" I screamed.

I had forgotten that every Saturday morning the landlady's 70 year old mother came to clean the house for a couple of hours. There she was, stood just ten feet away; looking like a Mrs Doubtfire clone with a Ken Dodd duster in her right hand. She didn't say a word; she just stared, looking me up and down.

I performed the most perfect pirouette, spun around and legged it up the stairs like a rat up a drain pipe. I leapt into bed and told Julie what had happened, she laughed hysterically. Oh My God!! I had some explaining to do.

I met with my landlady Gail on Sunday afternoon; it was a tense kind of meeting with lots of apologies from me. We both laughed out loud in the end but agreed that I should find somewhere else to live as my single lifestyle was a bit wild. This decision suited me fine as I had already found another place; my good friend

Ginger Chris was coming back to the UK from holiday repping and needed to live near Gatwick for his work, so the timing was perfect.

We would move into 6, Budgen Close at the end of the month, a house that would become legendary and be known as "The Ranch".

Week 4: Monday morning training.

On arriving in the classroom, we were introduced to a new girl who had joined our course. She was Irish and had started her training before Christmas but was forced to go home due to family problems. Her name was Lynn and she was very strange. The girls took an immediate dislike to her. (Six months into the job and she would be sacked for stealing £800 from the duty-free bar).

During the morning break she informed the group that she was an IRA sympathiser. This freaked a couple of the girls as during the weekend a mortar attack had taken place at Heathrow; she couldn't have come out with a worse comment. It is never easy joining a group of people who have already got to know each other but she was certainly odd.

On another course that had just started the previous week (course 95), there were three guys. Andy Blackburn, an excellent bloke who would become a member of the "Dirty Dozen", a name given to our group of straight guys in the airline, or the s.a.s. (straight air steward). The other two guys on Andy's course had slightly bulging eyes and camp wrist movements, I suspected they were gay.

We had been informed by the instructors that a grooming session would take place that afternoon. The lads didn't need to attend as it was all hair, make-up, nails etc and that we could go off and do our own thing (a bit of male bonding etc). Muskrat and I headed for the gym and then the pub. Meanwhile, Andy and the two guys from his course had gone to the airport to look at the planes!!

Apparently, as Andy told me, the three of them were standing on the gantry looking out to the runway, watching the planes taking off when he said,
"Isn't this great, all the girls stuck in the classroom and here we are, the lads, looking at planes and not a homo in sight".
The other two guys laughed uneasily and nudged each other behind his back. Both of them were as camp as Christmas but didn't want to let on. (They would

remind him of this day out at the end of the course, much to his embarrassment).

Things were coming together nicely on the course and the hazy, unclear picture was becoming more focused. I was moving into my new house that weekend with Ginger Chris and I received a letter from Corinne in Australia saying that she was missing me. We had also received our first roster for flying; each person would be paired with someone from our course for the first flight, for moral support I guess. After this we were on our own. My roster read: Newark New Jersey – Los Angles – JFK – Boston. Excellent, I thought.

The last week of the course was quite tense. As you can imagine, fail the exam at the end and you're out. Monday we were up at Heathrow in a local swimming baths, inflating life rafts and doing ditching drills (quite interesting really as a Jumbo Jet had never successfully ditched in the sea at that time). Three of the girls had also confided in us that they couldn't swim. Could be interesting I thought, as it was a CAA requirement that crew must swim 25 metres unaided.

As I stood on the edge of the pool, it reminded me of a Miss World Beauty Pageant, with Muskrat and me as the judges. The girls looked fab in their costumes. We jumped in, inflated the life jackets and got down to it. Those who couldn't swim we just held up or disguised the fact the best we could. Somehow we just about pulled it off.

Final uniform fittings were completed and we were informed that Richard Branson would attend the wings ceremony at the Park Lane Hotel in London. This was where the inaugural, pre-flight party to Hong Kong would be held. But first, the final exams.

Part of this exam included each potential cabin-crew member choosing a piece of safety equipment, then present and describe its use to the rest of the group .Example: "This is a fire-extinguisher; you use it on fires in a sweeping motion" and then explain the quantity, stowage and location, etc. It was all a bit nerve-wracking. Then it was my turn.

Janice, the instructor, turned to me.
"Oh Gary, the loud-hailer please" she said.
I picked up the instrument and smiled at the group, they had come to know me as a bit of a joker by now and laughed uneasily as I was about to start, not knowing what mad thing might just pop out of my mouth.
"Right everyone this is a loud-hailer. When the plane has ditched in the sea and you're bobbing about in your bright yellow dinghy, some of you will be in the water wearing bright yellow jackets. So when the

sharks start heading towards you because they can't miss you, wearing that gear, I will be on the loud-hailer shouting….Get the fuck out of the water! There's a shark behind you! By the way there are two loud-hailers on board the 747".

Everyone burst into hysterical laughter. Janice and Karen, the instructors, looked at each other, shook their heads and roared with laughter as well. It eased the tension somewhat and everybody finally got through their practical and written exams, some by the skin of their teeth.

Our wings were presented, photos taken and we were on our way. The pleasure ticket for travel and fun was about to begin

CHAPTER 3

MY FIRST FLIGHT

My first flight and I was a little bit nervous, even for me. Alison, from my training course, was with me and she hadn't slept too well the night before.

Before every trip a pre-flight briefing takes place. This sets the tone for the entire journey, safety questions are posed to the whole group, normally about 15/16 people, and if you get two wrong then you're off the flight, although this happens very rarely.

Things that are discussed during the operational briefing include…any famous people on board, flight times, special meal requests, safety updates, special-needs passengers, unaccompanied minors and seating. It's all very daunting at first but it soon becomes second nature.

The In-flight Supervisor (IFS), who conducts the briefing along with two Pursers, basically creates the atmosphere for the flight that is to follow. The standard and consistency of these briefings from IFS and Pursers varies dramatically, as I would discover over the coming months. Luckily Alison and I have fallen on our feet and everyone was very helpful; others from our course were not so lucky.

As I mentioned earlier, my only real fear was going around the plane with a teapot saying "anyone for tea" and sounding like a total faggot. A hostess friend of mine told me to grab the coffee pot when it came to that part of the service so that, when walking down the aisle saying "coffee" you should croak your voice up a bit and say "coorrfeee" quite hoarsely and you'll be okay. Good tip, I've passed this on to other people a few times.

The flight went well, no hiccups and we arrived at Newark. Once on the crew-bus the music was turned up, the ties came off, shirts and blouses were undone and it was time to start getting into the drink we had taken off the plane. 2 miniatures was the regulation…. yeah right!

On arriving at the hotel you collected your keys and flying allowances, 120 $ per night at that time or 200 $ for two nights. Good money really. It was a quick shave and shower, then off to the crew-room for a party. This place was normally tucked away in the hotel, to avoid disturbing other guests staying there. Basically the drinks flow and old flying stories are exchanged, everyone and anyone gets slagged off and as more drink is consumed, the stories get wilder, conversations more liberated and always end up with the topic of sex. "Spin the bottle" or" Truth or Dare" are the common games played along with "I have never". At this particular party the Purser working at the front of the plane in upper-class shouted out,

"I have never given a pilot a blow job".

A fifty-five year old Captain who hasn't said much all night suddenly pipes up from his seat,

"That is until tonight darling".

"Fuck off, no way, I don't do my own crew" she replied, got up and walked out. Everyone laughed out loud.

At this point I saw Alison having a cheeky glance at me; as I caught her eye she blushed. Aye up I thought, I'm in luck here and sure enough I was. As the party wound down, it's back to my room for a touch of heads down, feet back.

In the morning, upon waking up, I looked at Alison who was fast asleep and appeared so cute. I then gave God the thumbs-up and mimed "Thank you, nice one" with my thumb raised in the air.

On the flight home I came across a couple of flying procedures that were not in the manual.

At the end of the meal service, the Purser at the back in charge of economy, a lovely girl called Trish, told me to call the flight deck and ask the Captain to turn on the seat belt signs as we were about to collect the meals and too many people were standing around, getting in the way. I thought this was a little odd but carried out her instructions. Sure enough, the Captain duly acknowledged my request and the "Fasten seat belts" sign was illuminated. Trish explained to me that 350 people's meals to collect is a bit of a nightmare if they're all standing, or in the aisles trying to get to the toilets. So, on go the seat belt signs, out go the carts and in come the meals, nice and smoothly. Turn the blinds down, switch off the lights, turn up the cabin temperature, all the passengers fall asleep and we can have a seat, chill-out and its less work for all concerned. "Hmmm! sounds interesting" I can remember saying to myself. It was common procedure at the time and had probably been passed on for years (it was certainly going on when I left). These were pre deep-vein thrombosis years may I add.

On landing at Heathrow airport at 8.30 am after a seven hour flight, I was quite exhausted. It had been an intriguing first flight and I couldn't wait to get to bed. I also wanted to find out how it had gone for the rest of my training course colleagues. People who fly for a living will tell you that after a night flight, when your head hits the pillow, you are zonked and sleep so deeply for several hours that you are almost totally unconscious. (the best way to get over jet lag is to sleep for about four hours, get up early evening and try to stay awake till midnight. This helps your body adjust quicker).

On waking up, the phone started to ring, everyone from my training course was eager to find out how everybody's trips had been. As it turned out, not all had gone as smoothly as mine. Some of the girls had encountered "psycho-host beasts". These are female senior crew, in their late thirties/ earlier forties, who are in charge of the flights and are total bitches. They are basically bitter women, scarred by their failed relationships with other crew members. Hagged in their looks, they have a deep hatred for new, pretty crew coming on line, they see them as a threat with their good looks, fit figures and energetic disposition

A couple of girls from my course, Gemma and Ali, had been reduced to tears by one of these psycho-host beasts who had been giving them a hard time for being slow with a particular service on the flight. They were both deeply upset, Gemma said she was going to resign and that she didn't need that kind of shit for the money she was getting. I tried to reassure and convince them to give it at least four / five more trips before making that kind of a decision. After all they had trained so hard for the past six weeks. They agreed with me but I could tell that Gemma's dream had been dashed (she would resign two trips later after encountering a member of the "Pink Mafia"). What a waste!

Muskrat's trip had been much more like mine; however a homosexual Purser had made him an indecent proposition. Muskrat had told him in no uncertain terms that his arse was for "one way traffic only" and to take his face for a shit. Other girls from the course had encountered similar psycho-host beast experiences and were also very down. One of them had also been pestered all night by a frisky Captain who wanted her to go to his room for a Baileys coffee and a massage. In the end she had to switch off her phone.

Some of the crew had also been prey to practical jokes. One of the girls, Louise, (she was a bit thick) had been told to stand on the tarmac in Boston to count the suitcases onto the aircraft to make sure there was one for every passenger. How lucky I had been I thought.

CHAPTER 4

THE PINK MAFIA

With a couple of days rest under my belt I was ready for my next flight to Los Angeles, a place I was really looking forward to visiting (this trip would have a pivotal influence on my flying career). At that time the airline provided free transport between London Gatwick and Heathrow airports as some flights departed from each place. The buses ran every hour and were normally pretty full with crew members heading back and forth. The people at the back generally slept whilst at the front it was gossip city, who's shagging who etc. Many a relationship had come to an abrupt end after overhearing a conversation on those bus journeys, I can tell you.

The In-flight Supervisor on the trip was a guy called Barry, nickname "The Silver Fox". He was a small Scottish guy with a similar banter to Billy Connolly, very funny and a good person. Coming along with him was his good friend, "The Housewives Favourite" – senior cabin-crew Dougie Love. He was from Brighton, a good looking guy and as smooth as a shaven seal, he didn't walk he glided. Dougie also had a way with the ladies, making them feel they were the most important person in the room. Looks like Ted Danson from the T.V show "Cheers" were my first thoughts. Dougie was a senior and only worked in first class, looking after the rich and famous. Passengers flying to Los Angeles had to pay 5700 $ for an upper-class return ticket, a fair price in anybody's money. The Pursers on the flight were two lovely girls, Sue and Katy.

The briefing was undertaken in a positive, upbeat, professional manner and everyone was feeling motivated for a good flight. (Next time you fly you can tell if the crew have had a stressful pre-flight preparation and briefing. They are not as friendly and attentive as they should be). A couple of famous people were travelling on the aircraft that day, Little Richard, the music legend, and Billy Connolly, a childhood favourite of mine. The crew-bus picked us up from behind the Virgin check-in offices, a quick pass through customs and immigration (designed for processing crew only) and on we filed. The chat on the bus was all about going skiing when we got to LAX, Barry and Dougie "The Housewives Favourite" had organised a posse to go up into the mountains early the following morning. I was well up for that and couldn't wait to get there

This was a real party crew, and during the safety demonstration I got well and truly stitched up by Sue the Purser. I was demonstrating the seat belt operation to intently watching passengers and as I un-fastened the belt clip and opened it, hundreds of pieces of folded paper fell out like a confetti snowfall. The observing passengers loved it…. the life jacket had also been tampered with, a condom placed over the blow pipe and a Tampax attached to the inflation cord... I was dying out there in front of hundreds of passengers but they were enjoying my obvious embarrassment and with a bright red, flushed face I made my way back to the galley. Sue was doubled up on her jump-seat.

"You fucker" I shouted at her.

"Sorry Gary but I couldn't resist it, the passengers loved it and they will be a lot less apprehensive now, makes the job easier" she replied.

Sue was in her early thirties and apparently a bit of a player in her time, always playing jokes but a great character and very attractive. She handed me a comb from the amenity kit and told me that a person in seat 52 F had asked for one, since I was new and dead keen I marched down there to give it to him. As I approached and began my "excuse me sir" speech, I stopped in mid-sentence as I could see the guy was totally bald. As I glanced over my shoulder I could hear the laughter and giggling from the crew hiding behind the galley curtains. They waved at me. Fuck! They got me again! I didn't mind, it was all character building stuff.

The flight of ten and a half hours passed rapidly and with about an hour to go, I went up to the front of the aircraft to chat with Barry and "The Housewives Favourite". As I passed through the curtains dividing the two sections (economy / pure luxury) I observed Little Richard who was obviously the worse for wear from drink or some other form of chilling.

During a long flight like this a considerable amount of money is taken from duty-free sales, etc and it all had to be accounted for. Barry, being the Supervisor, was responsible.

I handed over what I had taken in cash and visa slips etc and I asked him how the famous people had been behaving. Apparently, Billy Connolly had been hilarious, telling stories and jokes during the flight, much to the amusement of the other upper-class passengers and crew. Little Richard was in the toilet every 20 minutes and appeared happy with himself. We chatted for a while about the flight and the pending ski-trip.

I loved this job and I couldn't be happier.

My crew jump-seat for landing was on the borderline where economy and upper-class cabins meet, so I could hear all the conversations that were taking place.

As we began the descent into LAX, sweets were distributed to all the passengers to help ease the pressure on their ears that occurs during landing. Billy Connolly blurted out to the crew member offering him a sweet "Yes please, but I'm not getting in your car", everyone around roared with laughter again. (I would find out over the coming years that not all rich and famous people would be as funny and as nice as him).

On the final approach to land, we appeared to be going a little fast and the plane bucked and dropped a little, causing passengers to tighten their seatbelts, knuckles started turning white and people gripped their arm rests more firmly. Bump!! We hit the tarmac and swerved to the left. Billy Connolly, who is not a good flyer, shouted out extremely loudly;

"The middle peddle is the fucking brake, Captain". You couldn't help but laugh.

Through customs and it was off to our hotel, which was situated in the affluent area of Marina del Rey, five minutes from Venice beach and about fifteen minutes from Santa Monica. On arrival it was the usual procedure; check into the hotel, keys and allowances handed out. Then hit the bar. The beauty of the LAX trip was that there were at least two crews there at any one time due to the two night layover. With 200 $ of beer vouchers in my hand (s.a.s. term for down route allowances) it was time to party. The LAX hotel had a wonderful bar within its confines and a legendary barman, Jim who had broken many a young virgin's heart. A giant piano stood at the entrance, something that a lot of airline crews hadn't realised was solely for composing music and not for other, sexual activities that took place in the early hours.

A juke-box positioned in the far corner was knocking out tunes and created the atmosphere that got the party started. Small circular groups formed, as crew members caught up on the latest hot gossip (mostly who's shagging who, have you flown with? etc.) During the early stages of the evening the flight deck usually stuck together, exchanging old flying stories about V1, V2, did I ever tell you about that landing into Madeira when I used to work for Dan Air etc.

They reminded me of a pack of lions on the Serengeti plains in Africa, occasionally glancing up to pick out a potential victim for later that night.

I chatted to Barry and Dougie about our crew and what beautiful girls they were. They both filled me in on some essential pulling tips when in a room full of beautiful cabin-crew. Dougie explained:

"Pick your victim early, don't try and keep three/ four on the go at the same time, you'll always get blown out. Then find out if they have a boyfriend, if they say "well sort of" or "I have but he's not here" or "well things aren't so good at the mo", etc", then you're in with a good chance.

Barry then butted in; "The thing is to try and separate the one you like from the pack, i.e., the girls stick together as they feel as safe as lambs in a meadow. It's a bit like the T.V show "One man and his dog", you need to send in the border-collie to separate the lamb (the one you like) from the pack and get her into your pen (bedroom)".

Fuck! There was a lot more than to this than meets the eye but these two were complete pros and I would learn a lot from them over the coming months/ years.

I pointed out to Barry a beautiful young lady who was standing chatting to a couple of girls, not from our crew but from the previous day. Before I could say "fiddle de doo" he called out to her and beckoned her to come over, I was dying. Barry made the necessary introductions;

"Gary, Emma. Emma, Gary." etc...

"Gary thinks you're hot stuff, he's just started, only his second flight, he doesn't know you like we do" Wink, wink, nudge, nudge! Barry and Dougie laughed at each other then walked away leaving myself and Emma to chat.

She was about 5 foot 6 inches, beautiful face, and blonde, with pert 34C breasts that were well on show for all to see. I was hypnotised by them but didn't want to make it so obvious by staring too much. We chatted and laughed at the stories I told her about my repping days and she filled me in on the doe's and don'ts of flying. We shared a couple more drinks, then Emma explained to me that if you do pull discretion is your best policy, deny everything as gossip travelled at the speed of light around this company. We were getting on famously and as I began to tell her about our pending skiing trip, she interrupted and asked me if I had heard about the hotel Jacuzzi. No, was the answer.

"Well, go to your room, get your towel and we'll have a dip, I'll meet you there in 5 minutes" she said, adding "Say nothing to the lads!" and she was gone. I chose my moment carefully and then did a Paul Daniels illusion, disappearing out of the bar and up to my room.

I grabbed a towel and with lightning speed legged it to the outdoor Jacuzzi. Emma was already in when I arrived and was obviously wearing very little.

"Come on then, get your kit off and get in" she said, raising her glass. In I jumped. It was beautiful, the temperature was about 100 degrees and the bubbles were lapping around us. We clinked our glasses;

"cheers!" One sip, they were down and we were starting the business. Before I knew it, my boxers had been removed and she was on top, riding away like a fiddlers elbow. This was great! About ten minutes later we were disturbed by security.

A 6 foot 7 inch black security guard stood there in front of us, arms folded.

'Sorry guys! Jacuzzi shuts at 9 pm, you gotta get out! "boomed a deep, harsh voice.

Yeah, no worries, I'm not arguing with you Mr King Kong. We gathered our things and ran back to my room for round two.

5 am the following morning and my phone was ringing. It was Barry and Dougie;

"The ski-bus leaves in twenty minutes, so get your arse down here you rascal" bawled Barry.

Luckily I had sorted everything out the night before so after a quick shower and change, I was ready. As I reached reception a fair crowd had gathered, drinking coffee and eating donuts while waiting for all the stragglers to arrive.

"Hey ho, Gazza the shagger" Barry exclaimed.

"Nah, not me, early night, so I could be ready for today's trip" I replied,

"Yeah right, come on, tell us the story about Emma and you" persisted Barry. I remembered what she had said and flatly denied everything.

We all piled into the minibus and set off on our two and a half hour journey from Marina del Rey to the Mountain of Big Bear Lake. Barry and Dougie held court in the driver and passenger seats, frequently changing the music channel and guessing the songs before they started. I was exhausted after the previous night, so I decided to grab a couple of hours sleep before we got to the mountain.

On arrival at the ski resort we made our way to a rental shop to get kitted out with all our equipment. It was a place that Barry and Dougie had obviously been to before and we were fast-tracked through the fitting procedure and on to the slopes in double quick time. Here we all were, on a beautiful spring morning with breathtaking scenery, clear blue skies and snow-capped mountains, it was perfect, just like a picture postcard; this was work and someone else was paying for it.

We all had the most brilliant day; it was one hundred percent relaxing. I spent most of the time skiing with a girl called Sue who had been with the airline about three years. Going up on one of the chairlifts she confided in me that she was a bit down because her boyfriend had been cheating on her while she was away on her trips. I sympathised the best I could but I didn't understand why any man would want to be unfaithful to her, she was gorgeous.

Skiing finished for the day, we all met at the bar at the bottom of the slopes for a quick, hot drink while the sun was fading from the sky and the temperature was falling rapidly. With rosy-red cheeks and shining eyes we all looked so refreshed and cheerful. We handed in our skis, headed for the minibus and sped off back to the LAX bar in our hotel at Marina del Rey. During the journey, Barry and Dougie found some music to relax us and soon most of the crew fell fast asleep. As Sue snuggled up to me and rested her head on my shoulder, she looked so peaceful. God, she was beautiful.

Back at the hotel Barry insisted that everyone should go to the bar for at least one drink and reminisce about our wonderful day. It was nearly nine pm and the crew that had just arrived were well on their way in the bar. A quick shower, a spiking of the hair and I was there with them. I ordered my usual favourite beer, Miller Genuine draft, and started talking to the barman, Jim, about our trip. At this point I noticed that Sue had walked in, a perfect size ten figure wearing black leggings and a pink jumper, she looked great. She had panda eyes from wearing her ski-goggles and I teased her about it.

Just about everyone made it to the bar that night and the drink was flowing as usual. After about an hour, Barry suggested that we should head down the road to the British-run karaoke bar. Everyone filed out of the hotel bar, leaving a couple of girls sitting there who were definitely fascinated by the smooth talking barman Jim and his well-rehearsed patter.

At the karaoke bar it was obvious that Barry and Dougie were regular visitors and totally brilliant, professional singers. They knocked out song after song to entertain the twenty or so crew who had ventured down there and a handful of locals joined in the party atmosphere. Suddenly the DJ yelled out;

"Next it's Gary from Virgin, singing My Way"

"What! Me?" I shouted back

"Yes that's right" Barry and Dougie both replied. As I am forcefully pushed to the front of the stage, the realisation dawned on me; I am probably the worst singer ever. I have a voice like a goose farting in the fog. As I reluctantly stumbled onto the stage, shoulders slumped forward, I took the microphone and the crowd went wild. (Karaoke, as I would find out later, is universally done by airline crew, particularly in Japan where the all locals think you are brilliant.) I proceeded to murder "My Way" like it has never been butchered before. Due to my past holiday repping experience, I just about got away with it by adding a few cheeky bum wiggles and pelvic thrust movements. On returning to my seat, looking slightly flushed, Sue kissed me on the cheek and laughed about my performance. It had been a long day and about midnight we all set off for home.

Back at the hotel we poured into the lifts and pushed the relevant floor numbers. Sue pressed number two. I was on the fourth floor but couldn't make it too obvious and get out with her, as Barry and Dougie knew where I was staying. Once in my room I franticly searched for the crew list and located Sue's name and room number on it, she was staying in room 204. I picked up the phone and dialled the number.

"Hiya Sue, its Gary" I said

"Hi, what's happening?" she asked.

"I was just wondering if you fancied a quick Baileys in my room. I didn't like to ask you in the lift because of all the gossip" I continued

"Tell you what, come down to mine because I've got some chilled wine" she suggested. Great!

By the time she had put the phone down I was outside her door. On entering her room the lights were already dimmed and chill-out music was playing from the radio. (I managed one sip of wine and then it was off we go). I think Sue had a lot of pent-up sexual frustration with her boyfriend at home and decided to take it all out on me. I wasn't complaining, she was insatiable and a night full of passion capped off a perfect day.

The following morning, I was meeting Barry and Dougie for breakfast in the Sidewall Café down at Venice Beach. They quizzed me about the previous night's conquest, but of course I denied everything. The lads continued to tease me and tried to prize any scandal from me but I held my ground. The conversation then moved on to flying and how it worked, the ins and outs and the little games that you had to play to plot your way through potential mine fields and obstacles that could obstruct a smooth and easy life. Barry explained to me that one of the major keys to success was to look after the person who was responsible for your rosters. You were allowed to request two trips a month; these were based on rank and seniority, the more senior you were the better the chance of getting your bids accepted for such trips. Barry then went on to describe that some were much better than others; for example, if you requested a Japan Narita flight on a Monday at the beginning of the month, being a three night trip you would get back on Friday and have the whole weekend free. The flying allowance which, after duty-free sales, came to about £500 was a fair amount due to the strong Yen conversion rate at that time. Then you should request a two night LAX at the end of the month, also on a Monday and the way the computer system was set up meant that you had every weekend free and received great allowances as well.

Dougie then added "If you are not very senior like yourself, having only just started, or you've recently been promoted like me, then the odd two hundred cigarettes and a bottle of aftershave or perfume to the person who is basically sorting out your life (i.e. your monthly roster) goes a long, long way to swaying those borderline decisions on seniority and bidding rights.". (I would discover that cigarettes and perfume were their own form of currency, that roster personnel always smelt nice and their friends and family could chain smoke until their hearts content, particularly around Christmas).

I found all of this information quite fascinating. I was taking mental notes on how to play the system as fast as my brain would let me. "That's it, it's all about playing the game" I said, almost summing up the conversation like a judge to a jury.

"What about the psycho-host beasts that some of my course members have encountered how can they do that and get away with it?" I enquired. I explained about the girls on my training course that had been bullied and treated appallingly by certain senior crew members.

Barry replied: "They're all part of the system unfortunately, there's no union so no back up and they're all well protected by the Line Managers above them, who are basically their close friends since the time they all joined the company together some years ago".

"But it's all wrong" I blurted out in frustration. Barry agreed, but added; "It makes me look good though. Once you've flown with a psycho-host beast and then you get me, it makes me look great!". Dougie and I broke into laughter,

"Very true" said Dougie. After a long and very interesting breakfast it was time for a stroll along Venice Beach.

As it was a Sunday, Venice Beach was alive and a fantastic carnival atmosphere prevailed, with performances from a mixture of local nutters, jugglers, singers, comedians and artists all adding a unique spice of life to this amazing place. I loved it; it was a great spectacle. We met up with a couple of girls from our crew and wondered down the crowded street. Suddenly a huge black guy called out to us

"Hey! You girls! I can see by the way you are walking that you haven't had one of my twelve inch hot-dogs today." Hysterical, we all cracked up laughing. What a place!

The return home is another night flight of about ten hours, depending on the time of year and the wind direction. The journey went very smoothly, only about seventy percent full with plenty of spare seats. On long haul flights like this you're entitled to a rest. The crew-bunk areas are located in the tail of a 747 or downstairs on the Airbus A340, and are used for activities other than just sleeping, I can tell you.

Barry, the In-flight Supervisor, said that if we didn't want to use the bunks then we could use the spare seats in upper-class, as it was half empty (wouldn't be allowed these days). Travelling on board that night were Barry White and his good friend Quincy Jones. Barry's voice was so deep that you could hear it reverberating around the upper-class cabins, keeping everyone awake.

After my very welcome two and a half hours rest, I ventured forward to speak to Barry and Dougie. We discussed several subjects and finally got talking about the "Pink Mafia".

"Who are they exactly?" I asked. Barry explained that during the early eighties, the gay community were trying to find identification and credibility. Certain careers were unavailable for them as they would be ridiculed and victimised, for example, the armed forces. So, as they gradually came out of the closet, many of them moved into the travel industry, in particular the airlines. As this company expanded and new opportunities arose, the gay employees were promoted through the ranks and into Head Office. Now, they were in charge of overall cabin-crew positions, training and recruitment. They then looked after fellow gay employees like a "family". The straight guys were well and truly in the minority, to survive alone would be very difficult, so you had to play the game with them completely. As I hadn't flown with any of the Pink Mafia members yet I was slightly worried about how you played the game when a Pink Mafia supervisor was in charge. Dougie advised me that the best way was to pay them compliments. "What! I'm not telling a gay bloke that he's got nice hair or a nice bum. N.F.W" I replied, Barry and Dougie both laughed.

"No! No! Not that type of compliment, just how good they are at their job, how well organised and professional the services run when they're in charge, and what a great PA voice they have" said Barry.

"What, A-level arse-licking?" I asked.

"Basically, yes" replied Dougie. To be truthful, I didn't fancy that much but I was very happy in my new found career and I would just have to cross that bridge when I came to it (which wouldn't be long).

I had just completed the most brilliant trip; skiing, back to back rough and tumbles with two great girls, met a couple of good lads in Barry and Dougie and had realised that I was actually learning two jobs at the same time – how to be a cabin-crew person and how to play the airline game. I wasn't sure if I would be able to handle it.

CHAPTER 5

FULL HOUSE

After a LAX trip, due to the eight hour time difference you are entitled to three days off. These passed by quickly and it was already time for my next flight – JFK New York. Travelling up on the crew-bus from London Gatwick to Heathrow I was informed that the In-flight Supervisor on this flight was a colonel in the Pink Mafia, a total wanker called Billy Mott. I was thinking to myself that he couldn't be that bad; never pre-judge anyone was always my policy. Sure enough this guy was an A-level prick. The pre-flight briefing that took place was horrific. It was like a Krypton Factor rehearsal. Billy was joined by the two people who were to assist him, an over-the-top queen working in upper-class and a newly promoted Purser, Jill; she was already a nervous wreck because of him.

He was about 5 foot 5 inches tall, with an awful, squeaky Scottish accent and stuck-out ears that resembled the FA Cup. He had a nasty, pedantic streak in him, was finicky and an all-round bad aroma betrayed his presence. During the briefing each person was looking at each other with raised eyebrows and were taking deep breaths as Billy recounted what he wanted from the crew on this flight, his likes and dislikes. (one of his dislikes was flight bags being carried in a certain way). I could sense this was going to be a nightmare journey. And it was! How very different to my two previous flights.

Throughout the services, poor Jill who was in charge of the economy cabin was constantly being harassed by Billy; "This isn't right, that's too slow" or "That PA was wrong". The poor girl was really struggling and unfortunately passed her frustrations on to us by taking it out on the crew. I tried to encourage her a bit and told her not to pay any attention to him. He was obviously a strange, complicated person, just ignore him and let it go over her head. I think she knew that I was right but having just been promoted she was trying to impress in her new position and prove herself to Billy.

He was taking full advantage of the situation, knowing she was nervous and new to the job and loved the mayhem he caused, everyone was fed-up and arguing with each other. The ambiance he had created was terrible, a totally stressed-out crew but he secretly loved it in a smirking, sadistic way. I just wanted to punch him and if he had come near me I think I would have done so. Fortunately I was working on the trolley with a beautiful black girl called Naomi; she had started with the airline about two months before me, a previous French Connection model and lovely person. We watched out for each other during the whole flight, keeping ourselves busy and out of Billy Mott's way.

At the end of this horrific voyage we made our way to the hotel. I felt like I had just done a fifty-five hour flight with four thousand passengers on board. I was mentally drained and so was everybody-else.

I kept on thinking; how could this guy be in charge of a flight, looking after a crew of young enthusiastic people, deliberately de-motivating them and causing havoc like that. (I am pleased now that I have put pen to paper and been brave enough to bring this issue out).

The crew-room at that time in JFK was brilliant, two large rooms knocked into one to form a kind of L-shape. After such a crap flight I needed a stiff drink. The station manager provided the crews with free beer in order to relax and unwind (Forty-eight bottles of ice-cold Budweiser were delivered each day - a nice touch I thought). Only four from our crew of sixteen made it for a drink, Naomi and me, the In-flight Beauty Therapist and one of the junior crew who was working in the front galley. The rest were too traumatised.

We cracked open the Budweiser and were joined by a couple of the flight deck. The conversation soon turned to the ordeal that had just taken place. I ran the details passed the Captain who listened intently to what I told him and also mentioned the psycho-host beasts that had bullied and upset fellow members from my course. After about ten minutes, I paused and waited for his reply. Captain Tim sympathised with me and the other crew members present. He went on to say that, as they spent ninety-nine percent of their time in the cockpit it was hard for them to comment.

Although the pilots worked for the same company, they were quite independent, had their own union and also had managers in place who were gifted with common sense and the ability to see the bigger picture and did not suffer from the selective memory syndrome that appeared to inflict our own managers. We debated the situation concerning the Pink Mafia, Colonel Billy Mott and other psychos for about an hour, it was like self-counselling really, and it was nice to know you were not alone in your thoughts about them.

After a while the conversation soon turned to sex, as usual. The In-flight Beauty Therapist asked if we had heard about the new competition called "Full House". No we hadn't, but our ears all pricked up simultaneously. She then went on to give details; "Well, a couple of straight guys known as the Scottish Widows have started a competition to see who could sleep with every rank in the flying pyramid. Starting with 1 – Junior crew, 2 – Senior crew, 3 – In-flight Beauty Therapist, 4 – Pursers, 5 – In-flight Supervisors, 6 – In-flight Trainers, 7 – First Officer, 8 – Flight Engineer, and finally, 9 – Captain. First person to take all nine wins the Full House prize".

The stumbling blocks for me would be the Flight Engineers as they were all blokes, a bit hairy and smelly, and at that time the two female Captains were no oil paintings either.

"Well, that's quite intriguing" remarked Captain Tim. (I think he was going to enter the competition).

After a few more Budweisers the party was coming to an end. The First Officer, Captain and the In-flight Beauty Therapist departed first, followed by the junior crew member- Liz, leaving just myself and Naomi in the room. We both had the hots for each other and as soon as Liz left we got straight down to it, ripping each others clothes off; we were both totally naked in about thirty seconds. I had never been with a black girl before, and Naomi was beautiful, she had smooth, silky, dark skin; she was like a panther, so slim with perfectly round, 36C breasts with which to juggle, this was heaven! As she pinned me down and got on top, she started moving her wonderful body in all directions (I had never been with a girl before who could rotate her hips from side to side and back and forth at the same time). This was a great moment and another thumbs-up for God.

The following day, Naomi and I decided to spend our time in New York City as the hotel was only about forty-five minutes to an hours drive away on the metro. We were up early the next morning which was quite easy to achieve due to the time difference, plus we also wanted to avoid the other crew, especially Billy. We hit New York about 10.00am and did all the usual things, visiting the Empire State building, the Twin Towers (which were still there then) and the Statue of Liberty; then we did a bit of shopping in Maceys and moved on to Canal street for all the fake tags, Prada bags and purses. We headed back to the hotel at about 4.00pm, it had been a great day out and I was really enjoying Naomi's company. I definitely wanted to see her again for a rematch so we arranged to meet at the up-coming duty-free party that was to be held at the Roof Gardens, a nightclub/ restaurant owned by Branson.

Before checking out I invited Naomi to my room for a quiet drink before the wake-up call and preparation for the flight home. We had a quick six of the best, trousers down sex session, and then it was time to get ready. Everyone met in the foyer of the hotel reception, occupying several of the large leather sofas that were arranged in a square opposite a small souvenir shop and bar area. We were all hoping that Billy would be in a good mood and had managed a good sleep to chill him out a bit: nothing could have been further from the truth. A couple in the room next door had kept him awake all night with their non-stop shagging and to make matters worse, after having spoken to his boyfriend in Brighton, he discovered that one of his Poodles had been bitten by a German Shepherd and needed vet treatment. He was in a foul mood, and boy! was this crew going to suffer. What a nightmare.

Once on the flight Billy Mott called everybody together for a kind of mini briefing at the front of the plane. He basically told everyone that the outbound journey had been a shambles, all of the crew were incompetent, apart from him, and several members would have assessments done on them as they weren't up to standard. What a way to de-motivate a crew before a voyage home. Luckily, as it was a night flight, the plane was only half full and most of the passengers wanted to sleep. The hardest part was trying to keep busy and not fall asleep as there was so little to do. Naomi and I talked for most of the trip about our lives and what we had done. I arranged to meet her at the duty-free party a couple of weeks later. The flight was terrible, even worse than the outbound sector. Billy loved it however, inflicting sadistic pain on all the crew, strutting around like a fat, pregnant duck.

After a trip like that, I felt the necessity to go back home. I wanted to resign on the spot, nothing could be worth that kind of punishment for the money earned (I now realised what colleagues from my training course had gone through, I needed to be around normal, non-airline people). On arrival at Heathrow I phoned my parents, described the details of the disastrous flight I had just completed and said that I needed to come up to the North East for a reality check and some therapeutic normalisation. I dumped my Virgin stuff at Budgen Close (The Ranch) and grabbed a couple of hours sleep before catching the train home.

CHAPTER 6

TAKING THE MICKEY

It was Friday and I knew that it would be a good night out, (everyone in Newcastle lives for the weekend), a chance to party and let your hair down. My Mum picked me up from the station at about 6.30 pm that evening; it was good to see her and she informed me that all the lads were up at the golf club, including Dad and his friends; they were all eagerly awaiting my arrival. As we approached the ninetieth century white farmhouse buildings that had been converted into a club-house, butterflies tickled in my stomach. It was good to be back, and I was looking forward to seeing everyone.

Into the packed bar I walked and a huge cheer went up,

"Hey, it's Gazza, the air-hostess" shouted a voice from the back.

"So how many pilots have you shagged then?" asked Steve Chapman with a huge grin across his face.

I turned crimson red with embarrassment.

"Yeah right, none of that going on with me, one way traffic" I replied. As I walked to the bar another voice called out:

"Watch your backs lads, airline steward coming through". As I brushed past those who were playing snooker, they all shuffled backwards towards the wall in quick, short steps, remaining stiffly upright.

"Go on Gazza, get passed us so we're not bending over to take a shot as you're walking by, we've heard about you airline staff" exclaimed Stuart. A huge roar of laughter erupted, I had to join in, I was getting a good ribbing but it was all in good taste.

At the bar I chatted with all my old mates about my newly chosen career and what it was like. I held centre-court as I reflected on the trips I'd done, the people and girls I'd come across and all the rough and tumbles etc. I could see that they were green with envy. I went on to explain about the last trip and how bad this Pink Mafia guy, Billy Mott, had been.

"Well Gazza, I don't know how you kept your cool, I'd have belted him" said Richie, a lifelong friend of mine.

"The thing is, the other parts of the job are so good, the birds and the different places you visit" I replied in defence.

"Yeah, but you've got to be nice all the time to all those kind of upper-class Muppets who are total arseholes, I couldn't do it, and as for that faggot Billy, well what can I say, there are limits to one's resistance and patience" responded Richie.

I had to agree that it was a kind of balancing act, keeping tight lipped, but also enjoying the benefits this airline lifestyle gave me. I loved the life. (However, it did get me thinking, dignity is everything).

One of the guys at the bar, Brian Hurst who is obsessed with watching documentaries, was trying to convince anyone who would listen to his mumblings about the fact that man hadn't been to the moon, the reasons being the lack of flag fluttering, shadows, materials not good enough, blah, blah, and blah!. Upon seeing me out of the corner of his eye he stopped in mid-sentence.

"Hey! Gazza!" he called out, the bar went quiet as Brian had a reputation of uttering classic comments with the most incredible sense of timing.

"This Branson character that you're working for, he's got loads of 747 Jumbo's so why's he trying to go around the world in a hot-air balloon?" he shouted out loud. Everyone burst out laughing at the same time, "Yeah, very good" I replied.

God, I loved being home in the North East, it was so therapeutic and normal. The people are great, so friendly and at least they talk to you. That's why I think Newcastle is so popular with stag and hen parties from all over the country; they get to meet really friendly people and are very well looked after (unlike some parts of the UK where I have lived and visited). After re-charging my batteries at home I was ready to face work, nothing could get to me, I was ready to conquer the world again.

CHAPTER 7

THE CREMLIN

My next flight was a three night trip to Miami, one of the best that we did at the time and a great place to party and catch some sun. The In-flight Supervisor was a legendary bitch from hell, Fiona McEwen, a chief psycho-host beast. She had an awful, squeaky Scottish accent, she glared when she spoke and was totally unpredictable, what a hideous bitch. She sounded like Mrs Doubtfire with a stick of dynamite rammed up her arse. The briefing was a disaster, full of stress and negative vibes (did these people never learn), it was as if they were wallowing in the quagmire of atmosphere they were creating. Fiona obviously hated the new pretty girls and was completely jealous of their bursting energy and good looks. Apparently, she had suffered a major heartache when she was blown out by a Flight Engineer or Pilot of some kind. She picked minute faults with the new girls' hair, make up, nails, everything. I felt like saying "Fucking look at your arse, you fat waddling duck". God, she looked like a very ugly version of a certain princess, with a hangover to boot.

With the briefing ordeal out of the way we collected our suitcases and made our way to the waiting crew-bus to take us to the aircraft. Luckily, on this flight most of the crew at the front were very experienced and had requested this trip together. The juniors in the back cabin were a mixture of fairly new and ready-for-promotion people. As we climbed onto the bus it was obvious that all of the experienced crew hated Fiona as well and wanted nothing to do with her.

A busy eight and a half hour flight with a full complement of passengers followed. Fiona did her best to interfere wherever she could, putting people on edge, making lots of negative comments and giving no encouragement whatsoever. What a bitch! She had tried to intervene at the front of the plane but the experienced crew and their Purser, Sue Kawling, had told her in no uncertain terms to foxtrot Oscar. So she thought she would try her luck in the economy section, where there was a less experienced Purser called Ella, a beautiful Danish girl. I had more or less come up to speed with the services by now; most of it was common sense so it was becoming easier, but Fiona made me very nervous, she was a frustrated has-been. With most of the service out of the way, I got chatting to Marcus and Sue at the front of the plane who were working in upper-class. They told me that a trip to the Bahamas, on a five million dollar yacht, was being organised but to keep it quiet as no-one wanted to invite Fiona along, she would only want to take over and would be nothing but a misery. A set of specially coded instructions were passed around the crew so that they didn't pick up the phone in their room by accident and be persuaded by Fiona to go for breakfast or to the beach for the day, etc. (let the phone ring twice, hang up and then dial again, this way people knew that it wasn't her). It was a bit extreme but absolutely necessary in order for us not to have to listen to that bitch for three days.

Once at the hotel, we collected our allowance, 229 $ for the three nights, our room keys and off we went. We arranged to meet at the pool for drinks within the hour. As the crew turned up it was pretty much - get the drinks out that had been taken from the plane, add mixes from the bar, form a circle and then start the gossip.

Most of it centred on Fiona and what a bitch she was. As we unwound and chatted about the next three fabulous days, the senior crew mentioned the point of not answering the phone and getting pinned down with Fiona for three days. The two flight deck guys who had joined us were kind of bemused,

"Fiona's surely not that bad?" suggested one

"Fuck me mate! She's a nightmare, she might be nice to you guys at the front, but she's a bitch from hell back there in the cabin" replied Marcus.

Marcus was a well built, handsome guy, who had been flying for about three to four years and was ready to move on into another career. He had no patience for the likes of Fiona and her kind and wasn't afraid to air his opinions. A good guy, and very likeable. At that point Fiona waddled over to where we had all gathered.

"Hi guys" she boomed out in her horrendous, squeaky, Scottish accent, "so what are we all doing over the next couple of days? I thought I might organise a day out, what do you think?" she continued.

A deafening silence fell over the group, (no fucking way I thought, you've been a bitch from hell all of the flight and now you want to enjoy the good part of the job, no way, that's not how its going to be). Sue, one of the senior girls, interrupted,

"It looks like everyone is doing their own thing on this trip Fiona" she said, winking subtly at Marcus.

"Okay, never mind" replied Fiona and then continued to make idle gossip with the Captain and his wife, who had come along for the ride. About seventy percent of the crew had brought someone along with them as this was a very good trip to do so. Before Fiona arrived, Marcus had sorted out the taxis into

South Beach that night for some heavy partying and the luxury cruiser had been booked for ten o'clock the next morning. Individually we made our excuses and left the gathering around the pool to head to the hotel foyer and off to South Beach for a mad night out.

Our first port of call was the Clevelander, a favourite bar with airline crew and a wicked place to hang out. The brightly coloured art-deco building was heaving with people when we arrived. There was a live Irish band knocking out some top tunes as we all headed straight for the bar and started getting into the huge choice of cocktails and shots. About twelve of us had proceeded down there and some of our group had brought a friend along for the trip, Marcus and I were the only guys present; Heaven! Ten women and two blokes, I liked the odds. Crawford and Craig, the other two guys in the crew, had gone off to the vibrant gay scene a few blocks inland. Phew!

It was quite obvious that one of the companions had the total hots for Marcus and lots of touchy feely stuff was going on very subtly. I was targeting the Purser Ella, who was Danish by birth and totally beautiful but I could see that one of the crew's companions was also up for it. Happy days! Nice having a choice I thought.

After several drinks in the Clevelander it was time to move onto the South American bar, Mangos, for some Salsa, Boogie and jigi, jigi music. Things were really moving here, Marcus was now in full flow with his potential victim, plenty of tongue tennis and lots of stroking. I was kind of bouncing around trying to make my move but not upset anyone in the process. That hip thrusting music does get your loins moving and the scantily clad in-house dancers were certainly adding to the spice of the night. After about half an hour in this bar I saw Marcus make his move and leave by the side door, he was almost gliding like a swan, unnoticed by everyone apart from me. Lucky bastard I thought.

A few more cocktails and it was time to move. As we trooped onto the pavement outside Mangos, the posse gathered together.

"Let's get back to the hotel and have a bit of a room party" piped up Karen whose companion had disappeared into the night with Marcus. "Hold on a minute! Where's my companion? Ali and Marcus?" she exclaimed,

"Well I think they've gone for a bit of rough and tumble" I replied,

"No way" replied Karen, "Ali's not like that, they've probably gone for a walk",

"Yeah! right!" I answered.

As there were ten of us to get back to the hotel we needed three taxis. Right! This is the moment. Send in the boarder-collie I thought. (I wanted Ella but one of the companions, Helen, was up for it as well). I grabbed Ella's arm,

"OK, we'll get this one and you guys can get the two behind" I said as we jumped into the taxi and sped off. About thirty seconds into the journey I leaned over and started kissing Ella passionately, this was great and her response was most encouraging. We kissed all the way back to the hotel which was about a ten minute journey. As we pulled up at the door the rest of the guys were already there, somehow they had beaten us back even though we had left first. Wiping the lipstick from our faces, we staggered into the hotel.

"Right, up to my room for a party and grab some drink" said Karen whose companion had still not re-appeared. Once in the room the usual crew party procedures kicked in, scrounged drink was put on the table, music turned up, the balcony doors which happened to look upon Miami Bay(very tranquil) were opened, those who smoked sparked up fags and flirty gossip started in small groups. Helen, one of the crew's friends, had been giving me the eye all night and started to make a bee-line for me, obviously the cocktails had kicked in and she was feeling much more confident.

It was the usual: so how long have you been working for Virgin, what did you used to do for a living, how old are you, single or married? You're so lucky being cabin-crew, I'm thinking of applying etc. All the time I was keeping one eye on Ella who was really fit, but Helen was also quite tasty and well up for it. I could see that Ella was flagging a bit due to the drink. At this point who should bound in but Marcus and Ali, and an almighty cheer went up

"He Yee" I took one look at Marcus and burst into fits of laughter, he was literally covered in sand from head to toe, including his knees.

"Where in the fuck have you two been? You're covered!" I shouted out.

"Nowhere" replied Ali, "we just went for a walk, didn't we Marcus?"

"Yeah right, you're covered in sand" I yelled out much to everyone's amusement.

"No! Well, we sat on the beach for a chat during our little walk" replied Marcus who was kind of smiling and grimacing at me to shut the fuck up. At this point I noticed that Ali's top was inside out and her label was in full view. I nudged Marcus and pointed this out to him; he turned bright red and burst out laughing as well. This timely interruption allowed me to break up my conversation with Helen and beckon Ella out of the room and away as she was clearly a bit tipsy. I took her hand and headed towards the lift.

"Look Ella" I said, "do you fancy a Baileys up in my room and a little massage, nothing in it of course" (which in crew language means: let's get upstairs and shag each other to death). "Okay, but no funny business, alright?" she replied,

"Yeah: Okay! Scouts honour" I answered. Back at mine the Baileys were poured, lights dimmed to romantic, music to Love FM and Ella was lying face down, her top carefully removed with baby lotion being applied in pepe la pu fashion. During the massage I told her how beautiful she was, smooth skin, beautifully sensual body etc.

"Tell me Ella, what do you like sexually?" I asked, curiously.

"Well, I just love receiving oral sex" she giggled. At this comment I performed a spectacular Torvil and Dean ice-dance manoeuvre and spun her over, removing her tiny panties with one flick of the wrist, and began to lick the most fantastic, bald, wet pussy ever. Two or three minutes into it and she was literally going berserk, groaning with desire, panting heavily and as she shouted out she was about to cum a huge torrent of juices flowed from her crevice, I thought she had wet herself. Ready for my turn now, I was dismayed when Ella gets up, dresses, kisses me on the cheek and advised me that she couldn't stay but the sex was great, cheers and see you tomorrow (she needed her own bed and legged it). Fuck! How inconsiderate! Mind you I had done it myself plenty of times to other people, what goes around, comes around.

The following morning it was breakfast and then off on the cruise. Just as I am about to leave the phone rang. It was Ella feeling terribly guilty about the previous night's activities as she was well in love with her boyfriend and had had a bit too much to drink.

"No worries Ella, I'm really discreet and I'll keep the whole episode under my hat."

"Ok great. Thanks" she replied

The cruise boat came into the docking area that is situated about four hundred metres from the hotel in the Miami bay area. It was absolutely fantastic, five million dollars worth of pure luxury.

"Marcus you've done well son" I said and patted him on the back, (Marcus had been on this boat two months previously and had organised this trip for all our crew, apart from the psycho bitch Fiona who had been kept in the dark). We boarded this beautiful vessel and set off on a perfect day, the sun was shining, the birds were singing and there was not a cloud in the sky. Everything on board was free, the drink, the food, the lot. Everyone had chipped in 60$ (times by sixteen, equals 1600 $) and it was well worth it. The Captain for the day, Jo, was in his late forties, with long gypsy, pirate-style hair, was well tanned, muscular and loved the scene; twelve cracking girls, four blokes (two of whom were gay), the odds were good. Fantastic! Jo began our cruise with a tour of the rich and famous houses around Miami bay; Hulk Hogan, Gloria Estefan, Don Johnson, Versace etc. It was all very impressive. The music was wound up and the drink was flowing, everyone chilling-out semi-naked on the 3 different deck levels. Wow! This was heaven, no doubt about that.

A quick glance at Helen in her bikini got me thinking. Hmmm! Unwrapped, she was much better than I had thought! She opened her eyes and saw me looking. Caught out, I raised my bottle of Budweiser.

"Looking good Helen, very good actually"

She laughed out loud and replied "And yourself!".

Should have a bit of a result here! Ella had not come with us as she was catching up with some friends in Miami.

Captain Jo, Marcus and I were on the top deck looking down on all the beautiful airline-crew babes topping up their tans. The two gay guys were in the worst swim-outfits you have ever seen, skin tight and well, nasty (ah well, they were harmless enough). After the tour of the rich and famous had passed, it was out to sea on the wide-open ocean. Jo floored the huge vessel and we sped off leaving Miami to disappear behind us.

This boat was spectacularly impressive and Captain Jo's assistant took us on a guided tour of the interior. Wow, how nice! The pièce de résistance was the master bedroom with a huge, circular bed and mirrors everywhere. "Any good?" I shouted at Marcus and then he leapt forward, jumped onto the bed and started shagging the pillow, how funny!

Back on deck Captain Jo had decided to take a break and drop anchor. Time for lunch and a few drinks and get the jet-skis out. We all gathered together on the main deck and toasted Marcus for organising this and to Captain Jo for being such an entertaining pervert. Lunch was served, beautiful!

During the cruise, we got the occasional glimpse of bottle-nosed dolphins and manete rays in the crystal clear waters. It was a most wonderful day. Captain Jo allowed all the crew and their companions to drive the vessel for a couple of minutes. A thrilling experience!

Later in the day as the sun began to set, we caught the edge of the Bahamas, the scenery was breathtaking and the water amazing. We took the opportunity to have a dip and flirt with each other; treading water with Helen and a couple of the crew, I commended her on how good she looked and she blushed a bit so I gave her a comforting pat on the bum, underwater so no-one could see.

Back on deck the drink was flowing, Bob Marley style music bellowed from the cruiser's stereo system. The sun was slowly disappearing and it was extremely romantic. If you can't fall in love witnessing this you never will. While Captain Jo was advising everyone that we were heading back to Miami, I chinked glasses with Helen; "cheers babe, what a great day". With the backdrop of a glorious sunset, palm trees, turquoise sea, multimillion pound yacht and free flowing drink, nothing could be better.

"Listen Helen, have you seen the interior of this beautiful boat?" I asked her teasingly.

"No" she replied

"Come on, it's mega" I said. Taking her hand we sneaked below without arousing any suspicion from her mate or anyone else, only Captain Jo saw us and gave me a wink and an encouraging, thumbs-up sign. Helen saw the huge circular bed, screeched out loud and we both jumped onto it. Before I realised what was happening, we were kissing and pulling each others pants off and then making really hard, passionate love.

It wasn't the longest session I have ever had but talk about explosive!! Ten minutes later it was all over and time to re-enter the main cabin, only to be challenged by Captain Jo who was tapping his watch and laughing; luckily no one else saw us.

It was dark when we got back into Miami bay, but it had been a totally thrilling day, a wonderful experience, Cheers God, I owe you one. That night Craig and Crawford have invited us to a club of their choice to go and chill out, gay of course (but not "too hard core" as they said). I didn't fancy it much but Helen and a few others wanted to have a look and thought it might be a bit of fun. It was called The Cremlin.

Eight of us pulled up in taxis outside the club, I had a bad feeling about this place from the start but in we wandered underneath a huge pink canopy. To be fair it looked pretty normal at first, a few empty cages, tanned, skinny boys in G-strings serving drinks. Little semi- circular booths were scattered all around where you could sit and observe the dancers as they came out. I positioned myself in one of these booths, right in the middle of everyone so nobody apart from our group could touch me or talk to me.

Crawford and Craig were obviously well known there and regularly waved loose-wristedly at people they knew and would then look and giggle bulgy-eyed at each other. As we observed the goings on I looked anxiously at Helen and jokingly said;

"Fucking hell, don't leave my side, this is not my cup of tea, and guess what? I need a piss!"

She choked hard, her shoulders heaving up and down. Anyway I had to go,

"Hey! Crawford" I called out to him as he was sitting at the end flirting with every man in there,

"What's the crack when you go for a piss? Do the gays use both the men's and the women's? What's the score son?" I asked apprehensively.

"Yeah no problem Gazza, use the men's and you might as well get the drinks in while you're up there" he replied, laughing and gesturing to Crawford. Well, I was in and out of that toilet quicker than Billy Whiz, think I nearly caught the big fella in my zip. At the bar I quickly ordered the drinks with a tanned, G-string man,

At that point I suddenly felt a presence on my right and as I turned to look, I stopped dead in my tracks at the sight before me! There, in front of me was a 6 foot 5 inch thing, smiling and staring at me, it had a handle-bar moustache, wore a bright red horse-riding jacket, stockings and suspenders, high leather boots and was holding a riding whip. On the top of his head was a black, spiked, shining, First World War German helmet. I was in total shock!

"Hi big boy, what's your name?" he asked, I was frozen, still in shock.

"Do you want to sit with my friends?" SSSHHIIITTT!!! At this point, I did a quick pirouette and shot over to my seat, smoke coming from the soles of my feet. Back at the table everyone was in fits of laughter but I was in a state of distress,

"Fucking hell, did you see that geezer at the bar? He tried to speak to me",

"Oh yes, that was brilliant, you're face was a picture" Helen blurted out between fits of laughter. Shortly after that I made my excuses, grabbed Helen and decided that it was time to go. Before leaving I glimpsed at Crawford and Craig who were in a passionate embrace. Fucking hell! The Cremlin, never again!

The following day was check-out day; this normally included a bit of a lie in, a couple of hours at the pool, a quick shop, channel flick the TV for two hours then get showered and meet downstairs. I did most of this but I had also arranged to meet Helen for a quick drink at the bar and then look around the shops. As we browsed in the gap store I couldn't help noticing how big the changing rooms were, I mentioned this to Helen and invited her to take a look. The moment seemed right, I started undressing and before I knew it I was taking her from behind, six of the best, trousers down, ye ha. Two pumps and a squirt; pulled a funny face and it was all over, great fun though. Another first time experience:

1. Sex in a Gap changing-room
2. Bedded on a multi-million dollar yacht
3. Visited a gay bar - The Cremlin Club.

At check-out Fiona had a face like thunder, she had just spent three days on her own but it was her fault, the miserable fucker. Anyway she was going to make us all suffer on the flight home. Upon check-in at Miami airport we had some disturbing news for the companions. The British Airways flight back to the UK had gone tech, so basically we would have a full load on our plane therefore there was not sufficient room for our friends on 30$ tickets (but that's how staff travel went sometimes). Sure enough the journey home was awful, but I kept saying to myself "just keep going, only eight and a half hours of hell and you probably won't have to put up with this bitch ever again" and with the experience I was gaining, it was well worth the effort.

There were only a couple of hours to go but Fiona was everywhere ,she was like a woman possessed, getting in everybody's way and continually interfering with all the services. She was scowling and mumbling under her breath, criticising pathetic little faults. As she scowled at me and made an unfounded comment, I'd had enough.

"Have you got a problem with me Fiona" I asked in a firm tone of voice

"No why do you ask" she replied

"Well it's just that you keep scowling at me and making derogatory comments" I replied.

"Ach, its' just that I get very frustrated when things don't get done exactly as I want and when I want." she replied in her hideous accent

I laughed out loud at her reply

"Fiona what a sad and lonely person you are" I said and walked out of the galley

CHAPTER 8

THE RANCH

I soon realised that the key to happy flying was to have a good home and a place where you could chill out and relax. The Ranch was certainly that. A nice, three-bedroom house, just two minutes from the Parsons Pig and five minutes from Gatwick airport, it was perfect.

Living with me was my mate Ginger Chris with whom I had worked together as a holiday rep for years.

He now had a job training animators to send out to the Mediterranean, (Mallorca and Corfu) to entertain the UK masses therefore he needed to be near Gatwick airport. Also in the house was Sam Derth who worked for an obsolete airline which always flew at 4 am in the morning, a real Mickey Mouse outfit. She had a kind of witch-like look about her and spoke with a Kenneth Williams high-pitch cackle to her voice

Nice girl though, claimed to be a part-time medium. She initially enjoyed the antics of Chris, me and our friends but eventually it would become too much for her and she would leave.

After my Miami trip I needed a massive sleep as I was off to London to the Roof Gardens for the duty-free party. Naomi was picking me up at eight o'clock that night so I had plenty of time. The beauty of coming back from a night flight is that you can sleep like a log, literally comatose with a bottle of water at hand in case of necessity. Six to seven hours absolutely unconscious, excellent! I had advised Chris that Naomi would be staying over after the party so as to be on his best behaviour; one important detail that I forgot to tell him: she was BLACK.

The party at the Roof Gardens was superb, loads of freebies from all the suppliers; Ray Ban, Gucci etc. Any company who sold products on the plane was there to promote their goods and keep all the cabin-crew happy as we had the direct contact with passengers during the flight. With plenty of free-flowing food and drink, lots of flirtation was occurring all over the place. With two carrier bags crammed with stuff, I decided it was time for Naomi and me to head for The Ranch. As we were about to leave Branson was on the microphone;

"Okay! The first girl to prove she has no knickers on wins two free upper-class tickets to anywhere we fly" and laid himself flat out on the dance floor. At that point a cracking blonde girl bounded onto the floor and lifted up her tiny mini-skirt to reveal all. Hmmm! Happy days!

Back at The Ranch and after a wonderful sex session with Naomi it was time to sleep. She told me that because she had afro hair, she had to wear a hairnet in bed during the night or she ended up looking like a scarecrow the next day, all spiked up and out of control. She looked well funny wearing it and made me laugh but a girl's got to do what a girl's got to do. During the night Naomi decided that she needed to visit the loo and, as I adjusted the bedcovers an almighty scream emanated from the landing; as I jumped out of bed Chris was screaming;

"Fucking hell, we're being robbed". He had bumped into Naomi in the corridor on his way to the toilet as well and because she is really black and was wearing her hairnet, she looked totally like a cat-burglar. As I flicked on the light switch she scuttled back into my room and I began to calm down Chris.

"Shit, she almost gave me a heart attack" he carried on, panting and shaking.

"Bollocks! I told you she was staying over Ginger" I shouted at him.

"Yeah, but you never mentioned that she was black" Chris whispered back, we both laughed out loud. Naomi left for her trip the following morning and we informed Sam of the previous night's escapade, she loved it, great fun.

Chris was off to Minorca later that day and informed me that one of his workmates, Terry the Terrorist, was coming over the following morning to stay as he was flying in from Greece and then off to the Costa B a day later. Terry was a great laugh, full of fun, a natural comedian, well that was his job so he had to be, but it would be good to see him.

CHAPTER 9

THE TAXI DRIVER

That night I met Philo Beddo and a few boys from the local Three Bridges footy team down at the Parsons Pig for a couple of swifties. I planned an earlier night after a hectic week and these boys were good for great banter. The following morning I was up early getting sorted for Terry to arrive.

He had flown into London Gatwick and was waiting for a taxi to pick him up. The familiar, cherry-red Vauxhall pulled up at the South terminal, Terry handed the driver his bags, jumped into the back of the cab and informed him of his intended destination – El Rancho….y rapido!

"So where have you been mate?" the taxi-driver asked.

"Corfu, working" replied Terry,

"Oh yes? So what do you do for work?" he asked.

"I'm in the entertainment business, teaching etc" said Terry

"Oh yeah, the performing arts, they're all gay aren't they? All those arty-farty types" replied the taxi-man.

"Well there are a few gay people in the industry yes, but not me, I'm not" Terry replied in his deepest, huskiest, most manly voice. For the next ten minutes he was desperately defending his sexuality to the taxi driver en route to the Ranch,

Yours truly was totally unaware of the conversation that had been going on.

I had hopped out of the shower and was drying myself off. On hearing the taxi pull into the driveway I went down to greet Terry in the true, jolly boy style, wearing only a tiny towel around my waist just covering the essential bits. I opened the front door as the driver was taking Terry's money and handing him his bags.

"Now then Terry you homosexual stallion, get your arse in here fast because I'm going to shag you to death".

Terry's face was a picture of pure horror and that of the taxi driver was pure disgust He scowled and frowned at Terry and muttering out loud "I fucking knew he was gay", revved up and drove away very rapidly.

Terry scuttled inside, the tail between his legs

"Gazza you fucker!" he shouted. He then went on to explain the conversation he had been having with the taxi driver and what I had said when he pulled in. We both fell about, it was pure brilliance.

As I was preparing for my night out with Terry I accidentally burnt the big fella on the iron. Ouch: that really fucking hurt! I had been watching the footie and not paying attention.

"Well that's you out of action for a couple of days, it'll do you good", commented Terry.

Fuck, I was really hurt and it definitely put me off pulling that evening, that's for sure. After a mad night out, I'd left Terry with a couple of crazy Virgin girls; he ended up going back to their house. He was telling me how weird they were, both had walkie-talkies and kept talking to each other through the walls when he was trying to penetrate one of them. He had a good night though as usual and leaving the following morning he asked me to pass on his regards to Ginger Chris.

CHAPTER 10

FLATMATE DISPAIR

In absolutely pure discomfort with my "penis on iron" injury, Philo Beddo advised me that the best thing to do was to get a tub of natural yoghurt and soak it in that. No sooner had he passed on his medical advice than I was off to Tesco at breakneck speed. On returning to the ranch, Chris was back from his trip so we exchanged stories of our exploits over the weekend; we were both doubled up.

As Chris hit the shower I decided to douse my penis in the huge tub of yogurt that I had bought and proceeded to have a nice cold beer at the same time. Sitting totally naked on the edge of the sofa watching footy on TV, beer in one hand, the remote control in the other and my penis dipped in yoghurt, this was truly relaxing. At that moment the lounge door flew open and Sam walked in and dropped her carrier bags. She had been on a seven hour delay and was exhausted; and there she was staring straight at me, a six foot, mad, Geordie bloke, totally naked, penis dipped in yogurt, beer in hand, watching the footy. At this sight Sam burst out crying and, legging it upstairs, slammed the bedroom door behind her. Hmmm! Interesting I thought.

After finishing with my yoghurt treatment I decided to put it in the fridge, after all there was about a litre of the stuff and I had only just bought it! Anyway I was off to play golf with Philo B and Scottish George. On returning to the ranch about six hours later Chris was up and about.

"Gazza, I think we've got a bit of a problem with Sam" he said,

"Oh yes! what's up? I enquired.

"Well, when you went out to play golf you put that yoghurt back into the fridge, right?"

"Yes" I said

"Well, when you slammed the fridge door shut, it tipped over and spilled all over the place including onto her salad that she had prepared before she went on her flight" Chris explained.

"Yuk! Oh fuck!" I said

"Yep, she went berserk, marigold gloves on, bleaching the fridge from top to bottom. Absolutely livid she was, said she'd had enough and that she was going to find somewhere else to live" he continued.

"Shit! That means we are going to need another flatmate". The only possible candidate for the Ranch who had the right credentials was the Muskrat! The accommodation situation would be sorted. But in the meantime I was off to Japan.

CHAPTER 11

THE CROW

It was the first time for me to go East and I was really looking forward to the experience. At that time the Japanese economy was booming so the down route allowance for the trip was massive, about £100 per night. Upon checking-in at Heathrow the first thing that you did was sign in, get your luggage label for your suitcase then see who was assigned as the In-flight Supervisor since this set the tone for the entire trip (you just prayed that it was someone good). Checking the list I noticed a name I would dread in years to come; "Sonia Patel" known to the crew as "The Crow". A Line-Manager and a total bitch from hell, she looked like a witch, she was evil, she hated men and pretty girls and I think at some point in time she had suffered a minor accident as now it was physically impossible for her to smile, so she just scowled permanently. She was on board to assess the In-flight Supervisor and a couple of the Japanese girls. Normally if you arrived thirty minutes before a briefing, you could check your e-mails; have a coffee and watch a bit of TV. Once we realised The Crow would be travelling as well, everyone was in panic mode. Crew frantically studied the S.E.P. (Safety Equipment Procedures) manuals, making sure all the newest updates were in place, girls were checking each others bright red uniforms to ensure all was in order including hair, make-up and nails.

As the clock ticked away, we were called into the briefing room. At the top table desk sat The Crow, scowling, staring each crew member up and down, observing their appearance, making the odd note and tapping her pen on the clipboard. Hugh Wild was the In-flight Supervisor and was obviously a little nervous but clearly seemed to be a decent bloke and made all the introductions. You could cut the atmosphere with a knife. The difference between the Japan/Hong Kong routes and the rest was the compliment of crew. Half was made up with nationals, in this case Japanese as they obviously spoke the language since 95% of the passengers we were taking to Japan did not speak any English. As Hugh began his briefing The Crow's eyes wondered around the room; she reminded me of one of Hitler's deputies, a look of pure evil in her eyes. At each briefing it was the duty of the In-flight Supervisor to ask set questions to make sure everyone knew what they were doing, if you got two questions wrong you were off-loaded from the flight. On asking the Japanese crew safety questions they pretended they couldn't really understand and would whisper the correct answers to each other in Japanese. Brilliant! I'm sure that Hugh was aware of this but he let it go as The Crow hadn't picked up on it. Also present as part of the crew was an In-flight Sales Coordinator. Since the Japanese had so much money they used to spend a fortune during the flights and sales could top fifteen thousand dollars, mad really, Gucci / Cartier scarves at a hundred dollars each were sold five at a time. On board as well was a guy from Middlesbrough called Woody who would become a legend in the flying industry (I would be the best-man at his wedding in years to come). I couldn't help noticing that Woody was wearing a shady-lady, grey overcoat (designed to keep the crew warm when we used to fly to Moscow in the winter), anyhow it was a giveaway signal of being gay. Kelly, from my training course, was on board; she looked about eleven years old with her tiny figure but had great big tits. Perfect I thought, this would be my target.

The junior crew, of which I was one, were split into two halves, one half working out of the front galley and the other out of the back. Woody, Kelly and I plus the Japanese were up front, the Purser and the rest of the juniors down the back; total number including Purser was nine. The senior crew looking after the upper-class worked out of the forward two cabins and upstairs and this was where The Crow was going to spend most of her time.

On boarding the aircraft and putting our bags and stuff away I mentioned to Woody about wearing the grey coat and that it was a tell-tale sign that he was gay. He was purely mortified and wasn't aware of it's significance as he had only been flying for about seven weeks. He told me that it had been freezing cold when he left Middlesbrough earlier that day. (Well don't wear it again!).

What amazed me about the Japanese passengers was how well organised and disciplined they were, they all marched on in single file, knew exactly which was their seat, where they were sitting, how to stow their bags etc. They were so different to the Brits who hadn't got a clue, took ages to board, sat in the wrong seats etc. Here, they all sat down neat and tidy, almost saluting saying "Oh we're all ready, let's go". So disciplined but brilliant!

The flight over was most interesting and without the help of the Japanese-speaking crew, who were brilliant, it would have been impossible. On flights to Japan the prices are fixed so all the airlines have to charge exactly the same price for economy and upper-class tickets across the board. Since it wasn't a price-driven market British Airways, Virgin and Japan Air were all on the same footing therefore it was important to distinguish through giving a good service so that the passengers would inform their friends etc and would choose Virgin as their preferred airline.

It was fun though, with lots of ad-libbing and chicken impressions during the meal service, quite hilarious. The Purser at the back in charge of economy was a bit of an odd-ball and was obviously a bit stressed having The Crow on board but she was keeping her distance for now.

During a break at the end of the meal service I was chatting to Woody and he told me that he used to be a prison officer but couldn't stand it any longer so decided on a total career change. He was 6 foot 2 inches tall with longish blonde hair and built like a tank. He had a soft northern accent and a handsome, Greek God like appearance (the women would love him). I had been advised by Dougie Love that in Japan karaoke was still massive and that's all people did. As we planned our up and coming nights out the curtain peeled back and in walked "Nick, the Babba Singh", a real character from Hemel Hempstead. He was a Cockney Indian and had some great stories to tell (I'm not sure how true they were, but very entertaining).

"Hey Nick, how's it going up there?" I enquired.

"That fucking Paki bitch is a nightmare, she's going to get my big "sheesh-kebab" up her arse if she ain't careful!" he replied, which was hilarious coming from Nick as they both had similar skin colour and ethnic looks.

"Interfering bitch" he carried on. At this point The Crow appeared clutching her clipboard,

"Haven't you got some work to do Nick?" she asked, scowling at him,

"Yeah, bye for now" he said and walked away. As The Crow walked in, Nick made a throat-cutting gesture behind her much to our amusement, then left.

"Hiya Sonia, you coming singing in Japan?" I asked trying to be polite by making small conversation.

"Well, I might" she replied. As she passed by and through the curtain into the economy section, she flashed her eyes at Woody and nearly smiled.

"Wow Woody, you're in there son, you're in with The Crow, fucking brilliant!" I said,

"No way, I'm not interested, I'm happy with my girlfriend" he replied.

"Listen son, you could make life easy for us if you kind of flirted with her a bit, give her the odd compliment or cheeky smile, it would go a long way" I added.

"No! No way, she's a dinosaur" he answered.

After that, the flight was pretty uneventful, each had three hours rest in the bunk-beds and three hours selling duty-free (long old haul to Japan). What we found a little unusual was the amount of Japanese passengers who smoked on the aircraft (in those days passengers still could). On arrival into Narita Airport, it was morning their time, so it was a quick drink in the crew-room and then kip, ready for a big night out.

Our first port of call was The Flyers Bar. It was packed with airline crew from all over the world, little square cubicles with seating surrounding a make-shift stage and a couple of large TV screens dotted around the place to project the words of the songs accompanying dodgy, cheesy videos. The beer they serve in Japan is a bit odd, full of added chemicals but after about three or four they suddenly make you feel mega confident and you think you can sing. So after a slow start to the night it suddenly got going and you couldn't wait to get up on stage and murder a few songs.

About 11.00pm it was time to take the bus to the legendary "Truck", an amazing place. The story goes that years ago a lorry driver dropped off the container from an artic-lorry during the completion of the airport at Narita. It's in the middle of no- where ,on a kind of mini motorway and someone decided to turn it into a bar for airline workers to go to for karaoke, get pissed and have fun. Although it's a unique place with a brilliant atmosphere, the toilets are woeful (Porter cabins basically). The owner had chartered a special, large Scooby Doo bus to go around the hotels and into Narita town to collect everybody. It reminded me of the mad bar in a Star Wars film, filled with odd beings from all over the world gathered in a truck container singing mad songs, and trying to get off with each other. It had a kind of surreal environment, unlike some Karaoke places that you go to where people are shy and kind of reluctant to sing. Here was a riot, airline crews trying to wrestle the microphone from one another.

The Crow arrived all glammed up, full war paint on and was on Woody's case immediately, he hated it. My progress with Kelly was going well and I couldn't wait to get those fantastic fun-bags out. Nick "the Baba Singh" had grabbed the microphone and was on stage about to sing "My Way". Suddenly he was surrounded by five Virgin girls who had decided not to help him as backing singers but to "de-bag" him, i.e. strip him naked. This was priceless! As Nick tried to sing the girls had pinned him down, off came his jeans to a thunderous round of applause, next came his bright orange, silk, Indian boxer shorts, the crowd went wild. Nick was exposed and his so-called large "sheesh-kebab" was out!! But it looked more like a very small "donner" to me! It was purely hilarious though and Nick, totally humiliated, ran from the truck outside. The girls then placed his orange Indian boxers that they had claimed as a prize, on the horns of the moose that hung on the wall behind the stage, this was marvellous stuff. After about ten minutes, Nick scuttled back inside, I handed him a beer and he reclaimed his pants to a rapturous applause.

"Nick, that was priceless mate, you alright?" I enquired.

"Fucking hell man, de-robed in front of hundreds of people and the "sheesh" was out son, the Hemel-Helmut out for everyone to see" he replied.

"More like the Hemel pencil, Nick" added Kelly, lots more laughter. After a few more songs and beers it was time to head back to the hotel. The owner of the Truck loaded up the bus with some very drunk airline crew and headed off into the night.

A minor scuffle had taken place at the front of the bus between Fiji Air and one of the Virgin pilots but it was handbags at five paces and no real violent manoeuvres. Back at the hotel it was party-time in the crew-room and more karaoke. The Crow was all over Woody, permanently trying to paw and kiss him and he was doing a pretty good job in fending her off. I decided that I had had enough beer and sing-a-long for one night and as I collected the room key from reception made a subtle move to the lifts taking Kelly by the hand. It was fun-bag time and Kelly would not disappoint.

The following morning when I met Woody and the rest of the crew around the pool, he looked a bit of a shell.

"So Woody, how did it go with The Crow last night" I asked,

"Disaster, I had to run off in the end and she kept knocking and ringing my room all night, I only had about an hours sleep" he replied. He did look worn out. Woody jumped backwards into the pool and swam a couple of lengths. As there were two crews there at anyone time it was fairly busy and idle gossip about who got off with who rumours floated across the pool in coded winks and nudges.

Woody was the first bloke I'd ever seen who was bald all over apart from his head, he had a fantastic six pack, a totally toned body and continually pouted, at one point around the pool I caught him looking at his reflection in a C.D disc.

"Jesus, Woody, you're so fucking vain" I said to him.

"My body is a temple" he replied, breathing in slightly.

"So do you wax your chest then, you homo?" I asked,

"Of course, this is the way forward now" he alleged, "Burt Reynolds, David Hasslehoff, hairy chests are out, bald is the future" he continued. We all laughed, this was typical piss-taking airline crew the day after a mad night out. We weren't the only ones looking at Woody; under an umbrella on the far side of the pool, out of earshot, The Crow was observing. She was like a panther in the trees, ready to pounce, staring the Woody down with dark piercing eyes.

Woody, Nick and I exchanged stories and reminisced about the previous night and prepared ourselves for a further night of riotous fun. Sure enough we got pissed again in the Truck. The de-bagging victim this time was a Virgin Flight Engineer called Dave Lawton. As he stood there on stage singing, he didn't flinch or struggle as the girls whipped off his jeans and pants. I'm not surprised; he was hung like a Grand National winner, what a weapon! As the party finished it was time to return early for check-out the next day and I knew it was going to be a struggle. As Woody had blown out The Crow during the first night she was going to seek revenge. She probably knew we had been out on the tiles again and would be feeling a little worse for wear the next day. She was right, we were hanging; my first flight with a full-Monty hangover and headache. Ouch, it hurt!!

During this sector The Crow decided to be a busy-body and was hanging around our galley like a bad smell, making notes and deliberately applying pressure. The Bitch! She decided to do an assessment on Woody which was none to complimentary, probably because he had blown her out, how vindictive she was.

On arriving back in the UK it was late afternoon / early evening. Travelling this way on a flight makes the jet-lag a lot worse. But with a handful of cash in my pocket and an interesting trip under my belt I was feeling pretty happy; plus the Muskrat was moving into the Ranch, so life was pretty good.

CHAPTER 12

"HAVE TICKET, WILL TRAVEL"

At this point in my career I was now eligible for staff concession travel. After you have been with an airline for a certain amount of time you are entitled to use the staff travel option, this was great, a fantastic perk, six free tickets anywhere Virgin flew and I only had to pay the tax (£30). What a bargain! The only downside being it was technically a standby ticket, so you had to wait until everybody else, i.e. full paying passengers had boarded the plane. You kind of feel like the lowest of the low standing there, but for thirty quid, who cares? Philo Beddo and Scottish George were along for the ride as the Beddo had his own villa in Orlando and was letting everybody stay free of charge plus a mate of his had the villa next door so, Happy Days! Here we were; four members of the s.a.s with our friends; Philo Beddo, Scottish George, Captain Tim Hiles and his lovely wife Barbara. This was going to be fun.

Since Captain Tim, who was Virgin's training captain and Barry, "The Silver Fox", one of the In-flight Supervisors who had been with the company since day one, were coming along with us, we were kind of fast tracked at check-in.

Upper-class seats were allocated plus the use of the first-class lounge prior to boarding. It just shows you; it's not what you know, it's who you know! This ticket would have cost two thousand, five hundred pounds one way, and here we were sat up front, fully reclined, drinking ice cold champagne and playing cards; Fantastic!

The trip to Orlando was wonderful! Golf everyday, trips to the legendary dolls-house, sunbathing, shooting guns at the range, it was magic and just what I needed after my first nine months in the flying industry. One night during the trip, full of drink I had told everyone how quick I was over one hundred metres and would bet anyone fifty dollars that I could win a race easily.

That was it; the following morning the Pepsi challenge was arranged and would be filmed by "The Housewives Favourite", Dougie Love. There we all were, warming up early in the morning like a scene from Chariots of Fire, the hire-van in front of Beddo's house was ready, engine revved up with the gate open, Dougie was doing the final settings on his video camera and the track had been measured by Barry, who would be the official starter. Several American families had been observing the strange events and had come down to offer their support and opinions.

All four of us crouched down and braced ourselves for the start.

"Three, two, one, go" shouted Barry. Off we sped like gazelles, I'm sure it was a false start but we were all legging it down the Orlando street. Little did I know that Joel, part of the group and a copper from Glasgow, was like shit off a shovel and beat me easily, a huge roar going up as he passed the finishing line, arms in the air. I was claiming a false start but no-one was having it, priceless and great fun and I graciously handed over fifty $ to Joel with gritted teeth. It was such a great trip and the company was fantastic. On the last night we headed for the dolls-house again and then a cheeky cruise through the Virgin crew hotel to see who was in town. The beauty of having Barry and Dougie along was that they knew everyone and were extremely popular.

On entering the hotel bar I was surprised to see a few familiar faces of people with whom I had recently flown .Conversations started up and the party was jumping, plenty of drinks and loads of good crack. At the end of the night we invited a couple of the girls back to the Beddo's villa for a night-cap. We had three takers, Dawn who I had known for ages, her mate Claire who was beautiful and a reluctant, fattish monster called Trish who was on her second flight and kept going on about her DJ boyfriend and how much she missed him.

As we left the hotel Barry decided to show off a bit and do a couple of screeching laps around the hotel forecourt in the huge station wagon we had hired. All of a sudden a police figure appeared from no-where and, flashing his torch and badge, beckoned Barry to stop. Luckily he had not been drinking.

As he was being grilled by the police guy at the front of the van, I couldn't help but notice that the cop bore a striking resemblance to Frank Cannon (a big, fat cop from an American TV show in the seventies and eighties). As I had drunk a few Budweiser by now, I couldn't resist shouting out.

"Oi: Barry, knock Frank Cannon out, the fat fucker, we've got a party to go to". There was lots of laughter in the van, Barry turned slightly trying to compose himself, I repeated my statement and the cop shone his torch into the van. Some quick, slick talking from Barry and he got let off, fortunately.

In he jumped and it was off to the Beddo's.

I was making great progress with Claire who was totally beautiful, we sat and chatted for ages, she was an ex-model and hairdresser, had a great sense of humour and was really sharp. Hmmm! I do like this one. Fat Trish wanted to go but Dawn and Claire weren't having any of it. We all advised her that it would be too expensive to get a taxi; no-one could drive as we'd all been drinking and Barry had gone to bed. Claire and I chatted and kissed all night. I think I was in love (think!! I later realised that I wasn't), She informed me that she had just finished with her boyfriend and that it would be good to meet up when we got back home.

CHAPTER 13

"MAD MICK"

When I landed at Gatwick after the break in Orlando, I switched on my phone and sure enough there was a message from Claire – this is my number, buzz me and we'll meet up. Thus the first real romance in my airline career began. Claire was awesome, a southern beauty from Cambridge and we got on great .Our first date was a West End show in London and then back to the Ranch for the best sex ever, everybody in the airline loved her as well as all of my friends at the Ranch. For the next couple of months we were inseparable and managed to swap onto each others flights, it was a wonderful champagne lifestyle (with lemonade money). I really loved it, one week in LA, the next In Hong Kong, it was a wicked time. We decided to take a five day skiing trip together in Lake Tahoe using our concessions. We flew from Heathrow to San Francisco – upper-class for thirty pounds, hired a 4 x 4 jeep for next to nothing and then up the mountain for a few romantic days in a log-cabin by the lake, which was amazingly beautiful. I had to admit that this lifestyle was irresistible and purely addictive. It was James Bond kind of stuff and you could afford to do it on limited funds.

I didn't think that life could get any better; after Christmas at my parents, New Year at Ginger Chris's, we were cruising, what could possibly go wrong? WHAT COULD POSSIBLY GO WRONG? EVERYTHING!

Claire and I continued to request trips together and were incredibly happy and inseparable. The weekend before our requested ski trip together with Barry, "The Silver Fox" and "The Housewives Favourite" Dougie Love, I had badly sprained my ankle playing football for the Three Bridges Football Club in Crawley, and had to phone in sick. What a nightmare as Claire and I had really been looking forward to it.

Claire phoned in sick as well out of sympathy so she could look after me because I was hobbling about all over the place. As it turned out I had been invited to meet Claire's parents for the first time and as we were both off sick this would be an ideal opportunity.

Her parents had invited us to spend a week at their luxury villa in Portugal for a bit of golf and relaxing so it would be good to meet them before the trip abroad. Now, Claire had been totally honest with me about her ex-boyfriends, or so I thought. As it turned out her immediate ex-lover was an extremely dodgy character. A white version of Mike Tyson and known as" Mad Mick" to all his friends, Claire had told me that she had called it off with him some time ago, but forgot to mention to me that they had brought a house together and it still hadn't been sold; also that Mad Mick wouldn't accept that it was finished. In his gangster world, He told you when it was over not the other way around. The two golden rules in life are:

1. Never get involved with a gangster's girlfriend, and

2. Never get involved with a gangster's girlfriend.

Claire filled me in on this minor detail as we were on our way up to her parents, speeding up the M23 in her familiar black sports car (she thought they were only minor, I was in semi-shock). She assured me that Mad Mick was history and that it was only a matter of time before the house was sold. I was happy with Claire but I was even happier with my own legs and the ability to walk unaided, not in a wheelchair for example. Fuck! I had this nagging feeling about Mad Mick and I would not be wrong.

As we pulled into her parent's house in Cambridge for the pre in-law meeting, the butterflies kicked in. It was a beautiful property, set in its own grounds and built into the side of a hill, so everything was upside down, with the bedrooms downstairs and a wonderful lounge upstairs with a sun veranda that looked out across the countryside. Claire's parents were out when we arrived so she gave me a fully guided tour. We then entered the lounge to look at photos of Claire when she was young and relax with a glass of wine.

We heard a car pull into the drive,

"That must be my Mum, she's been out shopping to get food for our dinner tonight" said Claire. As she stood up and walked to the window, the colour drained from her face.

"Fuck, its Mad Mick!" she shouted.

"Quick, hide, for fuck's sake, he'll go berserk" she continued in a panic-stricken voice.

"Fuck!", I'm thinking. Hide? Hide where? I don't need this, I love life and don't want to die at the hands of an ex-boyfriend called Mad Mick, why couldn't he be called Quentin and be as soft as shit. Anyway, my survival instincts kicked in and I hobbled downstairs to the en-suite bathroom in the parent's bedroom and locked the door (smart move, not)

As I sat there contemplating my fate, I hurriedly thought of the escape options available. I could hear the conversation upstairs becoming more heated and raised voices about Claire not being in San Francisco and what was she doing at home. At this point her Mum returned home and was obviously terrified at seeing Mad Mick there, knowing also that I must be somewhere in the house and not loving the situation.

As Claire and her Mum tried to calm Mad Mick down, he must have become suspicious and started thundering around the house, going into every room, checking cupboards and wardrobes as he went. Both women were screaming at him to stop, but he was on a mission. Suddenly the door handle of the en-suite bathroom where I was hiding, moved,

"Oh shit!" I whispered to myself.

"Who's in there?" he screamed, "Who's in there?" even louder this time. I sat there silently like a startled rabbit, motionless, praying, and waiting for Captain Kirk to suddenly beam me up to safety. Suddenly there was a thunderous bang as the door was totally smashed off its hinges. I stood up and stared at the sight in front of me, a giant, contorted figure of a man possessed,

"Who the fuck are you?" raged Mad Mick.

"I'm Gary and why the hell did you just kick down the door?" I replied in a surprisingly calm voice.

"Well, what the fuck are you doing hiding in there? What the fuck is going on?" he continued.

Claire butted in to explain that I was a mate of hers from work and had come over for a dodgy MOT certificate that her friend was getting me. Claire's Mum was shaking and obviously very upset, so I backed up Claire's explanation of who I was in the most convincing way possible.

We edged our way back up the stairs and into the kitchen, somehow distracting Mad Mick from wanting to kill me, temporarily anyway. As we continued to tell him that I was not her new boyfriend, it was starting to wear thin and I could tell. From the corner of my eye I noticed a very disturbing sight, ten meat-knives with gleaming silver blades and wooden handles, neatly arranged and looking menacingly sharp. Fuck! I needed to get out of there; I didn't think that he was going to buy this for much longer.

At that moment the kitchen door burst open and Claire's Dad rushed in. At last I thought. As the explanations were being exchanged I edged my way into the lounge that was separated by two glass sliding-doors. I positioned myself on the sofa and could hear the voices rising and falling, with lots of calm down commands being issued. I noticed a cordless telephone on the table next to where I was sitting and decided to dial 999. As I hadn't got a clue about the address, I was just hoping that the police operator would be able to trace the call from the landline number. Sure enough they could and assured me help would be on its way within the next five minutes.

As I sat tight a reassuring knock was heard at the front door. Two police officers entered the house. At this point Mad Mick made a sudden lunge through the sliding-doors, taking them clean off their hinges, glass flying everywhere and leapt towards me. As we wrestled to the ground the two police officers grabbed him in a headlock and forced him to the floor. Thank God, the ordeal was now over.

As Claire and her Mum were so upset after the incident, we decided to postpone the evening and her Dad ran me home. Talk about trying to make a good first impression, what a disaster! The journey home to the Ranch was somewhat muted but he did tell me that he had a nightmare with Mick as well and they had had a massive confrontation in his office after he advised Claire to finish with him (Mick had turned up, gone berserk and had wrecked part of his office).

The trip to Portugal went ahead but it was the beginning of the end for Claire and me. I had decided to move on as she had more baggage than a Samsonite sales person. I was young and doing a bachelor's job, I was a free spirit with a gregarious character and didn't need any full-time commitments, it was party-time and there were lots of fun and great trips around the world to discover.

CHAPTER 14

IN TROUBLE

For the next couple of months Muskrat, I and fellow members of the s.a.s would request loads of trips together and just enjoy life. The beauty of the flying industry is that when you are single, every time you go on a trip it's like being on Blind Date, only you have fifteen people to choose from instead of three. For the next three months it was blind dating all the way to the bar. A group of us from the s.a.s had decided to request a trip to San Francisco to hit the Napa Valley and do some wine-tasting. By some strange miracle, eight of us, all guys, had been rostered on the same trip, what a result! This was going to be some serious fun and heavy duty piss-taking with boys being naughty boys.

Along for the ride are myself, Muskrat, Simon R, Reading Andy, Zippy, Kieran, Paul Habbie Be and Ozzie Waine. As we all file into the briefing room the Purser and In-flight Supervisor are mortified at the sight of us all. (They can't even split us up as eight junior positions and eight guys). The briefing was fine with the final words being.

"Look guys, enjoy yourselves but remember that you have a job to do so don't go too mental", Yeah Right! Okay!

From the very off practical jokes and messing around were commonplace, Muskrat with a massive felt tip had drawn a huge pair of 38DD breasts onto Simon R's demo life-jacket and he hadn't seen it. Zippy was walking around with a condom on his shoulder, totally oblivious. The passengers began to board, filing onto the flight from hell. Zippy and Simon R were both brilliant at voice impressions including Frank Spencer, Zippy and George from rainbow, Frank Bruno, John Major and Chris Eubank amongst their expanding repertoire. As passengers took their seats the "welcome on board" PA was done in the voice of Chris Eubank, it sounded hilarious and the passengers and crew loved every moment.

The safety demo was a riot and when Simon R put on his life-jacket and a huge pair of breasts appeared a massive round of applause and cheering echoed around the back of the 747 Jumbo. God knows what the full-paying passengers thought of it all, it was different but great fun. During a spot of turbulence in mid-Atlantic the seat belt sign illuminated, this time it was the turn of Zippy who did the full PA in the voice of Frank Spencer, finishing with "has anyone seen my little baby Jessica".

Four hours into the flight, the Purser in economy had abandoned ship and had legged it up front to let us get on with it. At this point Muskrat has sprinkled icing sugar on four of the guy's heads and they were walking around looking as if they had severe dandruff and snow on their heads, oblivious to the joke. With such hi-jinks going on, the nine and a half hour flight passed in no time at all. The In-flight Supervisor and Purser breathed a huge sigh of relief as the wheels touched down in San Francisco. The welcome to San Francisco, thanks for flying with Virgin etc, was announced in the voice of Frank Bruno and the passengers gathered up their luggage and left the plane. After all the passengers had disembarked the In-flight Supervisor did the normal PA at the end of a sector followed by "remember guys, you are representing the airline down route so don't wreck the hotel". Zippy replied with a "don't worry" response from Frank Spencer and we all collected our crew bags and marched off the plane to commit a massive riot.

At the luxury crew hotel in downtown, all the essential amenities were on your doorstep. Once checked in and allowance collected, I made the necessary arrangements with the Concierge for our trip to the Napa Valley. A sixteen-seater coach had been ordered for eight am the following morning. Eight of us s.a.s boys from our crew and six girls from the previous day's crew were to make the epic journey.

An early wake-up at 7am and it's off for breakfast, we all gathered at the familiar Eddies diner opposite the hotel. For the pre- trip briefing, it was all the usual upbeat banter of airline crew, good one-liners, innuendos, piss-taking stuff.

Ozzie Waine who was a total lunatic had been to the liquor store the previous night and brought two cases of Budweiser for the journey ahead. Drinking Budweiser at that time in the morning isn't that appealing but you soon get used to it (believe it or not). Sure enough the bus turned up on time, typically efficient, American service. We all piled on, like a scene from a Carry- On film and it's off to the Napa Valley. The driver informed us that two more passengers would be joining us from the Marriott Hotel.

"What? You must be joking, two strangers with us maniacs? They'll hate it!" I protested.

"Sorry sir, that's my instructions" the driver replied.

"Jesus, that's a blow". Everyone thought that'd we'd have this bus to ourselves,

I wondered who was joining us. Two soppy yanks with no sense of humour I bet.

As we pulled into the Marriot Hotel forecourt, two slightly overweight individuals were standing there waiting, wearing chequered puffer jackets, dodgy, hound-dog ear furry hats and woolly gloves, this had got to be them. Sure enough it was. The bus doors opened and as they got on board they handed their voucher to the driver.

"Hi everyone, my name is Bill from Nebraska" said a portly gent in a cheesy American Twang. All of us looked at each other starry-eyed and just screamed and howled, followed in unison by our van chant:

"You're gay and you know you are, you're gay and you know you are". Bill and his 'wife' slumped into their two seats at the front of the bus and off we went (they must have thought this was going to be the worst day of their lives).

The journey up the Nappy Valley was great, over the Golden Gate Bridge, taking in a glimpse of Alcatraz to the right, which we were going to visit the next day and up through some wonderful, breathtaking scenery. The banter on the bus was pure piss-taking with rugby / football songs and chants. The Budweiser was flowing and Ozzie Waine, who was crazy, started his depraved repertoire of things he could turn his penis into, like a wrist watch, cheeseburger etc. everyone loved it apart from Bill and his wife who were thinking of getting a taxi straight back to San Francisco.

The Napa Valley and the wine-tasting were fabulous; huge, mansion-style, colonial buildings in beautiful settings, hundreds of bottles of wine for you to sample, all free. Before you could sample any of the wine though, you had to listen to a bit of spiel from a Nancy Reagan looking lady in her mid-fifties, who gave us a bit of history on the vineyard and the wines they produced. It was quite interesting at first but a bit boring by the fifth place we visited. As we stood there, all quite merry by now as we had been drinking Budweiser in between wine regions, the Nancy Reagan cheesy yank lady began her spiel on the history and wine etc for the fifth time. At the end she asked if anyone had any questions. With about forty of us stood listening to this presentation I stuck my hand up.

"Yes Mrs Reagan, I do", everyone looked at me in anticipation of what I possibly wanted to ask, and you could hear a pin drop.

"Yes, I've heard that the grapes you use in this wine are good for your piles, is that true?" I asked. A huge roar of laughter went up from the crowd. Nancy Reagan just looked at me with a thin smile.

"Gee, I don't know where you heard that from but that's not true" she replied oblivious to my wind-up question. That's the thing with yanks, their sense of humour and spiel is so different, everything just goes over their heads like a 747. It's very much like that when

111

you overhear them chat up a woman, it's kind of like "hi, I'm Brad, I earn three hundred and fifty thousand dollars a year so I guess you wanna sleep with me?" The British spiel is so much sharper and wittier, tongue in cheek stuff.

Back on the bus and it's time to head back to San Francisco for a mad night out.

Bill from Nebraska and his wife have disappeared by now and jumped onto another coach, Waines' penis impressions had become too much for them.

Back in San Francisco we had a quick shower, change and were up to the crew-room to meet everyone. A number of the crew from the day before and the fourteen of us who have just done the Nappy tour were dressed-up and ready to party. About twenty two of us in all, ready to hit a wild bar in San Francisco called "Johnny Madness", where you can sing, dance and stand on the tables, no holes barred. Taxis were organised in abundance for us by Steve the Concierge wearing the familiar dear-stalker hat and using his high-pitched whistle to attract the taxis attention.

Once at our venue, it was like a scene from a Wild West movie, everyone was well up for it; one of the girls from the other crew has attracted my attention. On making subtle inquiries I discovered that she was an In-flight Beauty Therapist, twenty five years old and semi-single (aren't they all?). She had a striking Julia Roberts look about her, her name was Justine Lake, but preferred to be called Lakey. She was well funny and sharp-tongued. As the night deepened I was making pretty good progress with salsa, hip thrusting dance movements and gyrations. As she headed to the toilets I decided to make a subtle move for her.

"Look it's quite busy out there and I really want to kiss you" I said and took her by the hand,

"Me too" she replied. We headed into the toilet cubicle for a quick rough and tumble. As the passion kicked in two heads appeared simultaneously over the top of the cubicle, bloody Waine and Muskrat. "Caught you!!" they blurted out.

Bastards! Purely embarrassed, Lakey and I head back inside to join the party. With base camp established I bided my time for our next encounter.

As the clock ticked on, the night faded away. All of the crew were copping off with each other everywhere, everyone from the s.a.s had pulled. Taxis pulled up outside the club and the crew disappeared into the night to exchange body fluids. I asked Lakey back to my room for a Bailey's coffee and a massage and we were off, round one of a romance that would flourish during the coming months.

The following morning was a scene of carnage, hangovers a plenty as we met for breakfast ready for

Alcatraz. As usual there were a few no-shows and it was the normal gossip of who, where, why, what with and the sexual exploits from the previous nights activities. I spent the rest of that day with Lakey, taking in Alcatraz, riding cable-car trains, and holding hands most of the time. As Lakey was leaving that afternoon we exchanged telephone numbers but not body fluids as she had a 'kind of boyfriend' and wanted to sort that out when she got back, but I told her I would buzz her on my return. After Lakey's departure I decided to get my head down for a couple of hours to re-charge my batteries. As I was sprawled on the king size bed and channel flicking trying to find something to watch without those eternal adverts, the phone next to me rang. It was Monty, a Purser with the airline, who had taken back the flight we had come on to San Francisco.

"Gazza, you're in deep shit! One of you lot drew a great big pair of tits on the demo life-jacket and when one of our crew was doing their demo they hadn't seen them, until the passengers burst out laughing. They had to stop the demo mid-way through as the girl wearing the jacket was so embarrassed. Anyway the In-flight Supervisor, Alistair "Tennis Ball Head" (part of the Pink Mafia), has reported the whole thing to Head Office so you're all gonna be called in as soon as you get back" Monty reported.

"For Fucks sake: What a nightmare! Cheers Monty, we owe you one for that" I replied. As soon as he had hung-up, I rounded up all of the s.a.s boys for an emergency meeting in the crew-room. When everyone had piled in I told them what Monty had said on the phone. A stunned silence descended on the room.

"So!" I went on, breaking the deafening silence, "what we need is a plan". For the next three hours we discussed all of our options and it was decided our only defence was to deny everything. We practised mock disciplinary procedures on each other, taking it in turn to be Line Managers and crew members. The only problem was Muskrat and Simon R, who had actually drawn on the jacket in the first place, were useless during the mock-up role plays and looked totally guilty.

As could be expected, that night's program of entertainment had to be put on hold due to the unforeseen circumstances.

"Fucking hell, Tennis Ball Head, what a jobs worth, just a bit of harmless fun that's all" was Ozzie Waines' finishing comment as we filed out of the crew-room at midnight

The following day at check-out, the In-flight Supervisors conducted a pre-flight briefing at the hotel, which was a little unusual. Head Office had obviously been in touch with her, basically all the s.a.s juniors were going to be split up on the way back, even though it meant that some of the senior crew had to work at the back and a few of us would have to work at the front.

Carol went on to advise us that there would be no crew rest as the bunk-bed facility was in op because the fire extinguisher was faulty. However, A-Zone at the very front of the plane was empty so if possible our breaks would be taken there; also that on landing at Heathrow all eight of us had to see the Line Manager before we left the building (not a problem for me as I felt quite confident at denying everything but I wasn't sure about Muskrat and Simon R who seemed very dismayed).

As it turned out the return sector services were fine, we were all good at what we did, after all we were quick, polite and intelligent people who just loved to have fun.

The Purser at the back, Sally, was obviously aware of this and sympathised with our high jinx activities on the way out (there was no need to take it any further, just a word of warning in the ear would have been enough, but Virgin thrived on incidences like this one. Disciplinaries were common place but common sense was not). As there was no union at the time it was a nightmare situation to be in as the management were judge, jury and executioner.

In my section at the back of the plane were a group of forty travel agents who had been out to San Francisco on an educational visit to learn a bit about

116

California and were well up for a party. As these were a good bunch, I had been plying them with as much free alcohol as they could consume and was receiving lots of attention from a very nice, tall, blond girl who every time I went past, flashed flirty smiles very seductively at me. Hmmm this could be interesting, I thought. With all the services out of the way, Sally had gone up to the front on her break leaving Zippy and myself to monitor the rear galley and to answer passengers' call bells etc.

I invited the tall blond girl whose name was Jo, to come and sit in the galley for a bit as the Purser was away on her break. As we chatted about San Francisco and what we'd been up to, flirting furiously with each other, Jo asked me that very familiar question

"So have you joined the mile-high club then?" she asked giggling and smiling,

"Well, not yet actually, but I really fancy giving it a go if the opportunity arose" I replied suggestively, "Actually Jo, the crew rest area at the very back of the plane is empty if you fancy a look in there?" I continued hopefully.

"Yeah, why not, you only live once" she replied. Great, I told her to go to the back where the toilets were situated and I would meet her there in a couple of minutes. I advised Zippy of my plan and headed down to the crew rest area.

Taking Jo by the hand we made our way up the spiral staircase and into the bunk-bed area. I slipped off my uniform shirt and trousers and took Jo from behind, hitching up her skirt up to reveal a tiny G-string which soon came down. This was great, so naughty but very exciting; if I got caught here I would be sacked instantly. Twenty minutes later and slightly flushed we re-entered the main cabin area (with my mile-high club certificate, ye ha). That was a great experience! Zippy had advised the rest of the s.a.s of my exploits, but all remained silent as they were more preoccupied with our pending Line Manager's meeting at Heathrow.

On arrival back to the UK we headed for the crew check-in area to await the Line Manager. Simon R went in first and admitted everything, so we were all free to go. Fair play to him, he was finally given a written warning and no promotions for six months.

CHAPTER 15

A STEADY GIRLFRIEND?

Back at the Ranch, Muskrat and I had letters waiting for us from Virgin; we had both been promoted to seniors meaning we would be working in the upper-class part of the plane with the nice big seats and very few passengers, instead of the zoo down the back with four hundred people. Happy days! It was time to celebrate with a party.

I had also arranged to take Lakey out on our first proper date. As she lived in Lingfield, Sussex we went to an evening horse-race meeting at the track there. It was a beautiful summer's night as we sipped champagne and lost our money but it didn't seem to matter, she was beautiful; wearing a short skirt, nice knee-length boots and a skin-tight top, breasts standing to full attention. It was time to head back to the Ranch and as we sped along the winding roads, roof down and music blearing out, I knew this was going to be a night to remember.

Body fluids a plenty! As Lakey groaned and gyrated up and down on top of me, a ghastly sight appeared through the glass panel above the door. As I looked up, a large, smiling, ginger head was nodding at me like a little schoolboy, giving the thumbs-up. Fucking Ginger Chris was getting revenge for me walking in on him and his girlfriend Jackie, the bastard! Lakey took it well and just gave him the V- sign; she was a lovely girl, great character and was going to be a very special person to me.

New Beginning

As it turned out Ginger Chris and Jackie, his girlfriend who had just returned from Greece, had decided to buy a house together therefore he would be leaving the Ranch in about four weeks. He had heard rumours that Jackie was having a fling with a Greek guy, Costas who ran boat trips, had panicked and gone over to Greece and begged her to come home with promises of many riches, house together etc. As it turned out Lakey was going to have to move out off her place in Lingfield as her friend was pregnant and Lakey's room was going to be turned into a nursery.

Even though we had just met, I asked her to move into the Ranch, to which she agreed.

CHAPTER 16

THE FIREWORKS

As a celebration for all these new developments we decided to throw a party of legendary proportions at the Ranch. It would be a firework party, hosted and compared by Terry the Terrorist. As it was July, the problem was that it didn't get dark until about ten pm and we lived in a residential area surrounded by hundreds of suburban houses with lots of animals and kids. Should we advise everybody of our intentions, answer: NO! As I scanned through the local paper I found a firework wholesaler in Lewes, just up the road from Gatwick, who should be able to supply us with what was required. As soon as Terry the Terrorist arrived at the Ranch we sped off to Lewes to collect our little bangers and rockets.

The fireworks place in Lewes was quite incredible, located in an out-building on a farm in the middle of no-where. We blagged to the owner that we were holding our display at a large country hotel with its own grounds. Inside it looked like a Vietnamese storage depot full of military hardware left over from a war; some of the rockets in there were six feet tall, different sized mortar tubes surrounded the whole building and large, coconut-shaped objects with long fuses protruding from them hung from the rafters. Terry was in heaven, he loved it; he was like a little boy in a sweet shop, skipping from box to box, chuckling to himself like a lottery winner. As he merrily filled our trolley, a dippy young girl was adding up what we had chosen so that we didn't exceed our budget; every time she looked away or got distracted, Terry would add extra fireworks underneath what we already had. As he looked for one last projectile, I suddenly saw the label on the side of a box - *six foot rocket, display rocket, the audience should be a minimum of 150 ft from this device.* What! Our garden was maximum twenty five feet long.

"Terry, read that" I said uneasily,

"Ah, no worries, we'll just point them in the other direction, at an angle" he said. Terry handed over the money and the deal was done. On our way home we couldn't hide our excitement and decided to stop and let one of the mortar fireworks off to see what they were like. Christ they were deadly, so loud, almost military; this was going to be an interesting night.

We had invited about fifty people, but word got around that the Ranch was having a party so more like one hundred and fifty people turned up and were crammed in like sardines. The audience was made up of mostly female airline crew and a few lads from the Three Bridges footy club as well as Muskrat's rugby friends.

Drink was in abundance, so much in fact that we needed two dustbins full of iced-water to store the huge amount of beer. Terry had brought along his company DJ system and placed two huge speakers in the window of Muskrat's room which looked out onto the garden,

He had carefully set up the mortars and huge rockets for the display. Everyone was ready and it had just got dark. Terry stripped off to his boxer shorts, lit the Olympic torch and went around the back of the garden to his pre-arranged starting point to begin his grand entrance accompanied by music from the movie Rocky. From the huge speakers the familiar de, de de de, from Rocky spurted out at top volume, everyone clapped and applauded as I shouted over the microphone.

"Let's hear it for Terry the Terrorist". As the crowd looked on all you could see was this flaming Olympic-style torch going up and down the back of the garden looking like it was lost and trying to escape, so funny. Eventually Terry bounded into the garden like a gladiator, held up his torch and the crowd went wild. He simultaneously lit the first rocket and mortar shell and beckoned the crowd to back up. As the missiles burst into the air and exploded the whole ground and street shook violently. Wow those fireworks were mental, so bright, so noisy, so powerful, and very impressive. After all they were industrial display fireworks. Midway through Terry's display a couple of mortars had exploded at the wrong height and a few custom-made rockets had entered the kitchen at high velocity, creating semi-panic amongst the ranks.

That was the least of my worries though, a mini posse of about twenty five angry neighbours were at my front door and not very happy.

As I opened the door, heart in my mouth, the angry group moved forward. Luckily I knew them all pretty well and with a quick, apologetic, slick spiel I managed to calm them all down, explaining that it didn't get dark until 10.00pm and I hadn't realised the velocity of the fireworks etc and it was nearly over anyway. As they knew I was a decent bloke and hadn't had too many noisy, frenzied parties since I'd been there, they dispersed back to their homes.

As they left one of the neighbours at the back gave me the thumbs-up and mimed out of sight of the others "LOVING IT!!!"

After the display had finished it was drinking, games, dancing, flirting and all the usual airline party goings on.

We also hit a few golf balls from the garden over the house roofs much to our drunken amusement (we later read in the local paper the following week that somebody walking their dog was nearly hit by a golf ball and thought it was very strange as the nearest course was 5 miles away and it was dark at the time).

The party finished at about five am. As I staggered around the house the following morning, it was a mess, bodies everywhere.

Muskrat had pulled Lakey's sister, God she'll be happy about that, not, I thought. Terry had legged it for a threesome with the walkie-talkie Virgin girls, lucky bastard; mind you he deserved it as he'd put on a cracking display of pure entertainment. The downstairs lounge was a bombsite, sprawling airline crew linked into each other, as if they had all been gassed.

Once in the kitchen I was joined by the Muskrat who looked ill.

"I see those make up artists did a good job on you Muskrat" I said

"Make up? On me?" he asked,

"Yeah, the rough as fuck look son" I replied

"God yeah, I'm dying" he chuckled

"Well son, let's get this cleared up and get ready for our seniors course".

CHAPTER 17

SENIOR COURSE

We had received the pre-senior crew course booklet through the post advising us of what we would be doing, i.e. the course would be three days long and cover all aspects of the upper-class service, how to do silver service, table lay-up procedures, what wines are served and the role plays etc.

The group would consist mostly of those survivors from my Training course, only about seven now, as well as people from just before and after; it would be nice to catch up with a few familiar faces. The course venue was at the Virgin offices in Horley near Gatwick airport. On entering the classroom we were greeted by a ghastly sight. The Crow had been drafted in as one of the trainers due to the airlines rapid expansion program. Fuck! Not that sour-faced, miserable git. Luckily the other trainer Dave was well chilled out and I had flown with him a couple of times before. As it turned out everything went pretty smoothly, apart from The Crow being her usual, negative, annoying self.

During one of the breaks a group of us had sat together at lunch,

"Is it me or is there something wrong with The Crow, or does she just hate everyone?" I asked

"No, it's not just you, she is just an evil bitch, loads of people have left the airline because of her; every time she flies she has some poor person in tears, totally out of order" replied Alison, a girl from my group.

"The problem is that we have no union so we have no one to consult, she's so well in with the Pink Mafia and the lot upstairs that you're just banging your head against a brick wall if you wanted to report her for the way she operates" I continued. We all agreed that it was out of order but the lifestyle was so good you just let it go as you didn't have to put up with it day in, day out. Once the course was completed and the one star badge awarded to stitch onto your uniform jackets, it was time to leave economy and move into first class.

CHAPTER 18

SHOCKING!!!

My first flight as a senior was to LAX, my favourite destination as there was so much to do, from skiing to sun bathing at Malibu, Venice Beach, Disney attractions, great golf courses, wonderful climate, great night life, the place had everything. Luckily for me the In-flight Supervisor on the flight was Barry, "The Silver Fox".

As I was officially working as a senior crew on the flight for the first time (although I had done this a couple of times before when people had been sick) I wanted to do well all the same.

The working positions were sorted out pre-flight in the briefing room and I was going to be working with a bad ass, mad geezer, Matt Channel, who was on his second to last flight and didn't give a shit anymore; he had enough of flying and was changing careers to sell cars at his Dad's Mercedes garage in Caterham. Barry, "The Silver Fox" warned me not to get tarred with the same brush as Matt and to keep my eye on him as he had a reputation for being very rude to passengers. Matt was a good looking guy, muscular with a loud London accent, very abrupt, confrontational and a larger than life character.

However, on this flight, Matt appeared to be on his best behaviour during most of the service. Working on the gleaming silver service trolley opposite him, we started the sweet and dessert service.

I was working the slow and Matt the fast end. Near completion, he stopped the trolley to serve a black lady who was wearing traditional dress that was exceptionally bright, typical of the colours they wore in the Caribbean. Matt pulled his sunglasses out of his pocket and put them on. Hmmm!! This could be interesting I said to myself.

"Hello Winnie" Matt blurted out in his loud, London accent. As the lady was wearing her headset while watching a film, she had not seen or heard him yet.

"Yes Winnie? It is Winnie Mandela isn't it?" he called out. I was dying on the other end of the trolley. As she removed her headset she finally acknowledged Matt's presence

"Yes well, as I was saying Winnie, would you like anything from the trolley?" he continued.

"Hmmm well, I'm not sure, what have you got?" she replied, oblivious of him calling her Winnie.

"Well we've got tea, coffee, possibly a BLACK coffee for you" Matt said, emphasising the word black, or some grapes? We have green or BLACK grapes, chocolates? White chocolate or BLACK chocolate" Matt continued, then paused and stared at the lady, hands on hips, sunglasses on and pouting his lips.

Before the lady could reply Matt suddenly grabbed the fruit basket and pulled out a giant yellow banana.

"I know what you want Winnie, a nice juicy banana" and he hung it from the zip at the front of his trousers, it looked extremely phallique!

That was it! I had to walk away for a moment to compose myself. On returning to the trolley the lady was asking Matt for a cranberry juice,

"Sorry Winnie, if it's not on the trolley you can't have it" and abruptly pulled the trolley into the galley. Once there, I stared at Matt in disbelief.

"Matt! What are you like? You can't do that" I said,

"Hey, you ain't seen nothing yet Geordie boy, wait till I get warmed up son" Matt answered as he headed towards the toilets.

At the front of the 747, in the upper-class section, a large semi-circular bar dominates the cabin, four bar stools are placed around it for passengers to sit, have a drink and a chat to pass the time on the long haul flights. Each crew member takes it in turn to work this position and then after about forty-five minutes is relieved to go and take a break.

At this time, Butch, a legendary gay crew member in the airline, was working the bar position. Three large American businessmen had gathered around the stools to chat about their trip to London and how successful it had been. Now Butch was so camp he would make Julian Clairey look straight and here he was, skipping around the bar, wrists in the air, dropping ice into the American businessmen's glasses, eyes slightly bulging with his bum stuck out. As he was serving them, one of them noticed his name-badge, "Butch" and signalled this to his two companions. As eyebrows were raised, Butch flashed his eyes at them, sucked in his cheeks and asked "slice of lemon sir?" In unison, they all declined.

Now Butch was not his proper name, but Colin. Butch refused to have his real name on his badge; he hated the Pink Mafia as much as anyone and had been turned down for promotions on countless occasions. The main reason for his unsuccessful promotion bids was due to one particular flight where Butch / Colin was making extremely good progress with a passenger who was also gay, lots of winking, touching of arms as he walked down the isle serving etc. Anyway due to new technology on board the aircraft, in those days it was possible to send individual messages to passengers' TV screens and turn them on or off etc. Butch decided to send a message to the guy he had been flirting with which read: "*Hi big boy, I want to give you a blow job in the toilet*". He entered the seat number and pressed go; unfortunately Butch sent the message to the wrong seat and an unsuspecting family, travelling with their twelve year old son, received it instead. Apparently there was hell on and Butch was lucky not to be sacked. He only kept his job because he'd slept with most of the Pink Mafia and had loads of juicy dirt on them, could have spilt the beans and ruined their careers (so he was allowed to use Butch instead of his real name).

As Butch continued prancing around the bar, much to the horror and amusement of the three yanks sat there, Barry, "The Silver Fox" went over to relieve him and Butch departed for his break. As Barry began tidying the bar he glanced up to see the three guys staring at him. One of them motioned Barry to lean forward as he wanted to ask him something. The Silver Fox bowed his head,

"Tell me, that Butch, he ain't so butch right?" asked one of the Americans. Priceless!! Barry laughed out loud, that was great!

Once into LAX, I had a great time, and a couple of days golfing at Industry Hills with The Silver Fox. When you have a girlfriend it seems that loads of other girls want to sleep with you, especially in the airline industry, and it's harder not to pull than to pull. I mentioned my concerns about this to The Silver Fox during one of our games of golf as Barry was all loved up as well.

The wise Silver Fox replied: "Why take a beefburger when you've got a fillet steak at home?" in his Sean Connery accent.

Hmmm! Very true I thought, mind you, a juicy burger doesn't half taste good now and again. What a job!!!

In between games of golf, I was privy to witness a fight between two gay stewards in the hotel bar. One of the guys had a bloke in every port of call and was also seeing one of the airline crew at the same time. On this particular occasion he had overbooked himself and there was hell in the bar. As the confrontation began they squared up to each other like inflated peacocks, cackling around the room in rapid, circular motions. Suddenly with arms raised high, wrists cocked at right angles, heads bowed, they lunged at each other, flapping their arms like out of control windmills; pure handbags at five paces. Priceless to watch, in fact I could have sold tickets for it, it was that good. As there was no immediate violent contact going on, everyone just watched and laughed out loud at this spectacle. After about ten minutes a couple of pilots jumped in to break it up as one of them was getting clumps of his hair pulled out and screaming like a banshee.

On our return sector from LAX back to London, we were really lucky as the upper-class area downstairs was only a third full, so it was going to be dead easy.

On the flight home, Matt was behaving himself after causing holy hell down in LAX. He was engrossed in a car magazine and the silence was golden, so Barry just left him to it; with only ten passengers to look after it was no problem. Most of them had decided to sleep during the night and had asked to be woken for breakfast with about an hour to go. Ice-cold orange had been prepared for them and the clock was ticking away.

Matt was suddenly on his feet and up to no good,

"Right Gazza, let me show you how to wake a rich bitch passenger who is sleeping, dead to the world" he blurted out in excitement.

God I had to see this! A lady in her mid-forties, covered in expensive jewellery was catching flies, in a comatose state, dead to the world and enjoying a peacefully deep sleep. Matt had poured himself a glass of ice-cold water, filled to the brim. As he tip-toed towards the lady I held my breath in anticipation of a disaster.

Matt dipped his fingers into the water and flicked the cold liquid into the lady's face and eyes. At first there was no reaction, so he repeated the process using more water this time. Suddenly the lady gasped and taking a deep breath, opened her eyes, obviously in shock and stared, eyes bulging, at Matt.

He put his hand down to the zip on his trousers, pretended to pull it up, let out a huge sigh and blurted out

"Ahhh: That was great, morning darling, breakfast is on its way" and jumped back into the galley. I stood there in complete shock. If I hadn't seen it myself then, I wouldn't have believed it. I thought this lady was going to hit the roof, but she just seemed to close her eyes, I'm sure she must have thought she was dreaming.

Matt Channel, what a bloke? Shocking!!!

CHAPTER 19

THE FLAMING DESIRE

Back at the Ranch I received two more shocking bits of news. Firstly I had bought a house, well Lakey told me that I had, with her, and that she might be pregnant.

Now I really was in shock. Wow, that knocked me for six. We seemed to make the move from the Ranch to our new home, in Maiden Bowers ever sprawling development, in double quick time. Before I knew it the carpets and curtains had been ordered, a double bed for the spare room and had signed on the dotted line. We also decided that we would need a lodger to help us pay the mortgage, to start off with anyway

As Lakey had chosen all the furnishings, down to the last knife and fork, it was only fair that I should be allowed to choose the lodger; who else but the Muskrat? Lakey's friends were mortified, saying that it would end up like the "Men Behaving Badly" house from the TV show, but I reassured her that it wouldn't.

With the move to our new house under our belt and everything running smoothly, Lakey and I were off on a three night trip we requested to Johannesburg, without the Muskrat. At the time, the trip wasn't a daily service, so twice a week a three night trip was available. It was an ideal opportunity to see a bit more of South Africa's beautiful scenery and spend a good time with Lakey. We had decided to go to the Kruger National Park and do a safari. The beautiful Sandton Sun Hotel, where we stayed in Johannesburg, allowed you to swap your room there for a luxury safari bungalow lodge in Kruger National Park; as it was part of the same hotel group. Pure luxury!!

As it turned out, most of the crew on the flight had the same idea, so in the end a posse of ten people headed up there. Johannesburg was so cheap and at the time seven rand to the pound was most inviting (it's about twelve these days, so even cheaper). As you were paid in local currency wherever you stayed, you could live like a king in South Africa and the money was pretty worthless when going back to the UK. (If you did have any rand left at the end of your trip you could buy cigarettes and flog them for a healthy profit on returning home).

After a three and half hour journey we finally arrived at the Kruger National Park. It is huge, an amazing place and totally unique and beautiful, plus our lodge accommodation was fantastic, five star. After checking in, we were huddled into large jeeps and set off for our first Safari adventure. It was dark by now as we set off into the pitch black wilderness we were all squashed very tightly into jeeps that had stepped seats. We did not really know what to expect, however two local guides accompanied us, one carrying a reassuring rifle and the other a huge spot-lamp/torch to guide us through the undergrowth. We couldn't see that much but the ambiance created by the animal noises was most interesting, hearing screaming howls followed by cracking branches made it all very surreal. By the time we had finished our first night's safari tour, we were all exhausted and it was time for an early night. We had to be up and ready to go at five-thirty am the following morning, as this was the best time to see the animals.

Sure enough dawn broke and it was a truly amazing sight down at the watering hole, watching all the wildlife in their natural surroundings. After about two hours we had literally seen everything, a cheetah, elephant, lion, buffalo, and wildebeest, everything except leopards. A quick bit of brunch and it was back onto the jeeps for the afternoon stint, we were kept amused, in between sightings of animals which were now becoming rare, by Kate, a really thick brummie hostess who kept asking ridiculous questions; for example,

"As the park is seven thousand feet above sea level, would we get turbulence in the jeeps?" she asked.

When she was told how many animals there were in the park, she wanted to know who had counted them.

I told her in jest "Its' Colin the counter who does it".

"Ugh, is that really his name? What a boring job Colin has" (straight over her head)

"What type of Lion is that?"

"Oh that's a 4.2 litre V 8 Lion" and also various other ridiculous questions about elephants and why they attack and rape rhino and that someone should keep an eye on them and stop them doing it.

For about two hours we hadn't seen much, the sun was beating down and it was about one hundred degrees. Suddenly a large African bull elephant was spotted dismantling a huge tree, Jesus, if it can knock that down what chance have we got in the jeep? As we approached with extreme care, cameras at the ready, the elephant got the hump, shaking its head violently and let out a huge "go away" noise from its trunk, it looked to me as though it was going to charge. Andy Blackburn, a member of the s.a.s, was in the back of the jeep with us. Suddenly he stood up and pointing at the elephant, started to sing:

"We're Reading, we're Reading and we'll kick your fucking head in", a truly verbal assault on the animal, just like he did at Reading FC football matches. Everyone burst out laughing, including the two guides. But the elephant didn't like it and made gestures towards us that made our guides do a full jeep reversal procedure to get us out of there.

With a thoroughly entertaining day of safari out of the way it was time for a party. That evening all of the guides who were there on the safari performed a cabaret, telling stories of how the park came to be open and how it integrated the animals with local people, all performed in full, traditional feather costumes around a large bonfire. It was brilliant and after a few jugs of wine and castle beers most of the crew were exhausted.

Lakey advised me that she was going to bed as we had another early start organised for the following morning, I told her that I wouldn't be long but I was going to have a few drinks with Andy to discuss football and England's chances in the World Cup. As you can imagine, with two lads talking about football in the middle of the African bush around a camp fire, drinking free beer, it wasn't long before the footy songs started. They were mostly Andy's about Reading FC and occasionally one of the black safari guides would suddenly blurt out "Bobby Charlton" much to our amusement. After another couple of beers I told Andy

I had a brilliant idea, I was going to jump through the fire naked.

Well, that was it, Andy was on his feet marshalling the safari guides around to bring more logs and wood for a marvellous spectacle that was about to occur; a typical Geordie cabaret was how he put it. Sure enough new logs arrived and as they took hold the flames were about ten feet tall.

This was it; full of drink which was making me feel very confident, I performed a couple of last minute preparations, a few stretches, touching of the toes etc, a quick check to see which way the wind was blowing and I was ready. Andy had produced his camera as this one was not going to be missed and he got all of the safari boys on their feet shouting my name "Gazza, Gazza, Gazza". I stripped off totally naked and sprinted like a white Linford Christie, tackle out, hoping the big fella wouldn't get singed in the flames and as Andy's camera flashed, I leapt through the towering flames and out the other side. I had done it, brilliant!!

Everybody fell about laughing, it was priceless, black safari guides doubled up on the floor screaming and banging their hands on the ground, belly-ache laughs echoed around the fire. I have to admit it was a sight to behold and probably would never be seen up there ever again. I got dressed, bid goodnight to everyone and headed back to my lodge where Lakey was fast asleep. I couldn't just wake her up and say

"Hey Lakey, guess what I just did? Jumped through the fire, butt naked, in front of fifteen safari guides, full of beer"

No I would tell her in the morning.

It was another really early start but, since I had consumed a few too many beers the previous night, the alarm clock was not a welcome sound. Lakey was already up and getting dressed.

"Come on we've got early breakfast this morning" she shouted in my ear.

I turned over and hugged my pillow,

"Lakey, you go and get breakfast I'll be down in a mo" I said rather tiredly.

As Lakey closed the door behind her, I suddenly had a flashback of the previous night's episode. Fuck!! I had better get up and get down there, Andy's bound to have told everyone and Lakey will go mad.

I hadn't had a chance to tell her about my fire leaping exploits. After rushing around frantically to get ready, I entered the breakfast area still half dressed.

I heard Lakey shout "he's done what?" The room was full of laughter.

Andy had just given a full, detailed account of last night's events. Lakey scowled at me like a prize champion in a "gurning" contest

"You are a small child" she screamed and pushing me aside, walked out.

142

Once on the jeeps again Lakey refused to talk to me and I had to sit on my own at the back, Billy no mates.

"No one loves me" I kept saying in a sympathetic tone.

"That's because you're a small, spoilt child and a disgrace" replied Lakey.

As I looked around for some support the bunch of safari guys kept smiling, shaking their heads and giving me the thumbs-up. So at least my heroic efforts hadn't gone unnoticed. Totally bored and with the last day of the safari out of the way we headed back to Johannesburg.

My leap through the fire story had spread like wild fire, pardon the pun, around the other crew members in the hotel, much to Lakey's annoyance; I wasn't bothered, just a bit of harmless fun I thought. I had got a reputation as being a bit wild but not nasty, just full of fun and mischief.

Eventually Lakey started talking to me which was lucky as we were off to Australia on holiday once we returned to the UK

Flying back from Johannesburg on a night flight I had plenty of time to reflect on my life and in which direction it was going. I was pretty happy with matters and wondered what adventures were around the corner.

I have to admit that the South African passengers were very demanding and very abrupt, slightly ahead of the Americans.

CHAPTER 20

FEELING GUILTY

The trip to Oz, via Japan, was only costing one hundred and thirty pounds, a great result. Although it was standby we managed to fly to Japan in first-class and were treated like royalty. That trip brought us both closer together, I had life cracked, a beautiful girlfriend, a cushy job flying the world, my own house, nice car, cool family and friends. Where could it all go wrong?

Well it would all start after returning from Oz and being called out for a night stop to JFK (New York). That's where it would all go wrong!

New York was your run of the mill trip, standard service, a night stop and normally you did one of these trips every month on your roster, or would get called out for one like me. The difference now was that we had a code-share agreement with Delta Airways, so two of their American crew would be flying with us on all our routes to the US. Now these guys were total characters, a lot older as well (average age about forty-five) and they took no shit. They had union back up which was exceptionally strong, so even if you murdered someone it was almost impossible to be sacked, unlike us where you were almost always looking over your shoulder and discrimination and lack of common sense were all too familiar.

With the briefing and pre-flight stuff out of the way we were on our way.

On board with us today from Delta were Marcia, a black, chunky flight attendant, quite a character and Steve, as camp as Christmas but very pleasant. Marcia however, took no prisoners and didn't suffer fools gladly. Word has it that on the training course merger so that they could fly on our flights, she had told Branson that, in her opinion, he was a womaniser and a bit of a rascal.

On New York flights the American passengers can be a bit in your face and abrupt, especially the youngsters who rarely say please and thank you and this really winds up the British crew beyond belief. Generally, on these journeys you will usually get a few curly-wurly passengers, i.e. the Orthodox Jews who have to have special kosher meals, (which take twice as long to cook and are a pain in the arse); some of them even refuse to sit next to women.

146

It is not uncommon either, to see them praying profusely at the back of the plane, stood up, bible in hand, head going backwards and forwards, like a nodding dog. As the Delta crew have union back up they're not afraid to give as good as they get if a passenger is being extremely rude, whereas the British crew would generally say: "yes sir, no sir, you're absolutely right sir", so that a complaint letter wouldn't be sent in and disciplinary procedures undertaken.

On this particular flight, Marcia was having trouble with a passenger, who couldn't have his first choice of meal, this was pretty normal on all flights to the USA. From the three choices on the menu, chicken would normally run out first and sure enough this American guy wanted chicken. Marcia's handling of it was priceless and her fearsome looks added to the proceedings.

"Listen sir we only carry so many chickens on board, there are no more! Now if I could I would stick my arm out of the window and pull a chicken out of the sky! Pluck all its feathers out and serve it to you, I would, but I can't!! After all this is a 747 and not a Seven Eleven, so do you want beef or vegetable?" and she glared at the irate American down her tiny rimmed glasses perched on the end of her nose. That was great; a British flight attendant would never have got away with that. Also on board was a striking looking In-

147

flight Beauty Therapist who was giving me the eye big time. During a break in the services I got a bit of time to chat to her. I found out she was single, had been flying for about three months and her name was Tara. She looked a dead ringer for Brook Shields and even when I informed her I had a girlfriend who did the same job as her and that we had a house together, it didn't put her off obviously flirting with me at all, in fact it made her worse. The rest of the flight was pretty uneventful apart from Marcia abusing a passenger who was stretched out in her crew rest seat thinking it was empty. Delta provided a special passenger seat as their crew must have a break after three hours in the air. Even if it was a dead busy sector, they would just down tools, go and sit down and there was nothing you could do about it; the union backed them all the way.

Once at the familiar cabin-crew hotel in New Jersey, the usual arrival procedures kicked in. Up in the crew-room there was a surprisingly good turn out. The Chinese banquet had been ordered and the beers were flowing. The usual airline conversations were starting up of who's shagging who, have you met such and such, had a famous film star on my last flight, total wanker etc. All company gossip. I decided to bail out early as I had organised a trip to the locally renowned Jones Beach the following morning for a bit of sunbathing.

With breakfast out of the way, ten of us piled into the crew-bus and headed down there; the rest of the crew, as per usual, were off shopping. Tara, the In-flight Beauty Therapist, really wanted to come with us but was meeting up with family friends and spending the day with them. Although only about a forty minute drive from the hotel, once on the beach it felt like a mini holiday. It was July and exceptionally hot. New York was reeling from a heat wave and temperatures were already ninety degrees. Six hours of pure relaxation, it was like heaven, nine beautiful girls and me. I felt like a king and kept getting jealous looks from bodybuilding Americans, who must have thought I was super loaded to be surrounded by so many gorgeous ladies; like a Hugh Heffner of the airline.

Bronzed and glowing it was time to head back to the hotel for pre-flight relaxation procedures which normally ran in the following order; room service, channel flick the TV for two hours, fifteen minutes sleep, shower and then check-out. On arriving in my room the familiar, red flashing light on my phone alerted my attention, indicating a voice-mail message; probably Lakey. As it turned out, it was to advise us that the flight was delayed by two hours so check-out would be later than scheduled; quite welcome after a long day in the sun.

As soon as I put the phone down it rang, surprisingly it was Tara enquiring about our day at the beach and wishing she could have joined us.

"Yeah, it was good fun but I burnt my shoulder a bit though" I said wearily,

"No problem, I'll come and put some cream on it for you and you can tell me all the gossip" Tara replied and hung up.

Hmmm! this could be interesting. Two minutes later she was at the door, I jumped from the bed and let her in. She was beautiful, stunning in fact and such naughty eyes. We started some small talk conversation and Tara asked to see my sunburn, as soon as I took off my t-shirt it just happened. Kissing! Passion! Frantic panting! lust and carnage. The chemistry was phenomenal. Before I knew it, we were making the most passionate love. Now Tara was every guy's dream, great looking and so vocal, loud screaming, panting and extreme gushing, what a combination.

At the end of the session we were exhausted and collapsed onto the bed, sweating profusely and bodies glowing, how good was that? When Tara left my room to get ready for the flight, the guilt kicked in big time. What was I doing? I had Lakey who was ace, beautiful and everyone loved her; my parents, my friends, and the whole world. Why would I want to jeopardise that? What was wrong with me (my aunt had the answer, I

150

was quite simply a man!) and men just couldn't resist temptation, especially under the circumstances I've just described.

Feeling guilt-ridden on the flight home, I spoke to Tara about Lakey and how great she was and that it shouldn't have happened. Tara was as cool as a cucumber and assured me she wouldn't say anything and that we should meet up when we got back, just as friends. That suited me fine and although she was a hot girl, I should have stayed away. After all I had Lakey. What a disaster it would be.

CHAPTER 21

A FEW EXTRA HOLES

Back at the Ranch 2, Muskrat had just got back from his Miami trip. I was going to confide in him about the voyage I'd just done but decided to wait for a more appropriate moment. It was early morning and Lakey had just gone shopping so it was pure peace and quiet in the house and time for five hours unconscious sleep. She had left a little note for me and a bottle of water by the bed, what a girl?

After a wonderful, coma-like sleep, I was just about to take a shower when I heard Lakey thundering around the house. She'd been called out for a Hong Kong flight and was well pissed off as we had planned a nice weekend together but that's the nature of the airline industry. Like ships that pass in the night I kissed Lakey gently on the cheek, squeezed her hand and she was off. This meant that Muskrat and I would have the house to ourselves for the whole weekend and that could be disastrous.

We arranged to meet all of the usual suspects down at The Frog House Farm Pub which was only a five minute walk from the house. It was a beautiful summer's evening and hundreds of people had gathered outside the pub to enjoy a few drinks and catch up on all the gossip. It was a terrific place and very popular with airline crew, the landlord had moved from the Parsons Pig to The Frogs and they had followed him in their droves. Our little group had formed a circle and were talking passionately about football, golf and rugby, the banter was great, totally relaxing.

As it was my round, I headed inside to sort out the drinks. As I squeezed through the crowds, who should I bump into but Tara, with whom I had just been to New York. I kissed her on the cheek and started chatting about the weekend and the wicked party atmosphere that the pub had.

The conversation soon moved to Lakey and I informed her that she'd just been called out for a Hong Kong flight. Tara's sparkling eyes lit up; "Hmmm!" she said flirtingly "that could be interesting!" She told me she was heading to Brighton with a group of friends from her course and asked me for my mobile number, stupidly I gave it to her.

I made my way back outside, tray of drinks in hand, to a torrid abuse from the lads about how long it had taken me. Switching the conversation back to sport the banter continued. The night passed with lightning speed and before I knew it Muskrat and I were walking back to the Ranch Two, singing rugby songs. We were like the "Men Behaving Badly" boys and the five minute walk took about thirty minutes as we kept throwing each other into bushes.

Back at the house my mobile phone beeped the familiar tone to let me know I had a text message, it was from Tara! The night out in Brighton hadn't quite worked out so she was getting the train back and asked me to pick her up the following morning, suggesting we should drive somewhere and take advantage of the wonderful weather. Dilemma! What should I reply, "Okay, why not?" I replied. (What an idiot!)

The following morning I told the Muskrat I was off to play golf with Philo Beddo, packed the clubs into the car and headed off to collect Tara. The roof was down and the tunes were blaring from the sound system. It was a beautiful morning, not a cloud in the sky, life was good I thought as I picked up Tara. She looked amazing in a short, pink, summer dress that enhanced her figure beyond belief. As we headed through the quaint, winding, country roads, she touched my leg and smiled at me with her fabulously naughty eyes. She looked good enough to eat. As we dropped down around a sharp, left-hand bend a huge cornfield came into view.

"Wow, look at that Tara" I said,

"Stop the car, let's go and have a look" she replied. We pulled over onto the grass verge, grabbed a blanket from the back of the car and headed into the cornfield, which was about four − five feet high. About thirty metres into the field, we flattened down the corn and placed the blanket on the ground, this was mad. We stripped off totally naked, sun beating down and no one could see us (unless they possessed a helicopter). We had wonderful sex, so passionate and electric. We lay there for a while then continued on our journey to the beach. What a day so far! We passed Arundel Castle and then on to Selsey, to a wonderful beach there. Even though I felt guilty it was so exciting and such a great day, we sunbathed for hours holding hands; giggling and laughing about nothing in particular.

As the sun began to lose its heat we headed back home. The air was still nice and warm and it was a beautiful early evening. We called into a quiet country pub, grabbed some food and enjoyed a bottle of ice-cold Chablis. Back in the car we were speeding along the country roads, listening to music when Tara motioned me to stop the car, leant over and whispered in my ear,

"Let's do it here, on the bonnet of your car, I really want to" very excitedly,

"Yeah: No problem!" Yab a dab a do! I hitched up her short dress, eased her on to the bonnet, put her legs around my ears and had sex again! Wow, this had been some day.

After dropping off Tara, I was back at the Ranch 2 and the Muskrat was watching TV,

"Fucking long game of golf that was" he said smiling,

"Yeah, had a few extra holes" I replied uneasily

"Come on Gazza, what have you been up to? Tell Uncle Muskrat" he said digging for the cause. I took a deep breath and blurted out the lot, every last detail of the last few days.

"Gazza, you're fucking mad, if Lakey finds out she'll cut your balls off, you dick head" he exclaimed,

"I know. What the fuck am I going to do?"

CHAPTER 22

A BIG TIME MESS!

The Sunday chill-out time had begun. A full Sunday lunch at the Hillside pub, followed by an all day drinking frenzy. Now Brighton wasn't my scene but somehow I had ended up there, at the Honey Club Sunday night special. At this time drugs weren't my scene and I was happier on the drink but ninety-nine percent of the audience there were off their nut. Somewhere along the way during the night, we had managed to gather a mini posse together and invited a few people back to the Ranch 2 for a night-cap and a few drinking games. Muskrat and his good rugby friend Scottish James had pulled a couple of naughty Virgin girls who wanted a ménage-à-trois and were taking all-comers. Muskrat was up for it but I wasn't feeling the love that night and guilt-ridden about my exploits I was not my usual self. Back at the Ranch 2, music turned up, the drink was out and the party got going

Captain Kev, a pilot with Virgin, (which is hard to believe as he is so wild) was in full swing, doing the splits and generally being a big kid. I'd seen enough for the night and motioned from the lounge that I was going to hit the sack, a rare early night for me. I occasionally heard the odd voice or laughing echoing up the stairs but apart from that I was dead to the world.

The following morning as I headed downstairs a horrific site confronted my eyes; the lounge was a mess and Lakey's nice new carpet ruined. Fucking hell! I screamed at Muskrat to come down but no response. I headed up there and two naked girls were either side of him,

"Muskrat; Get the fuck up!" When he awoke and saw the damage to the carpet he looked genuinely mortified. I was upset but what would Lakey say? We spent the whole day tidying and cleaning, moved a couple of tables into strategic positions and hoped Lakey wouldn't notice. Yeah right, no chance!

The day she got back, Muskrat and I were both flying off and had morning check-ins. Muskrat left well early as he didn't want to face Lakey's wrath on the damaged carpet front. She was due back anytime now and my heart was beating faster as the clocked ticked away. As I was ironing my work-shirt the door burst open and in marched Lakey, towing her black Delsey suitcase behind her; she had a face like thunder. She

158

collapsed into the armchair and glared at me, her eyes were furious.

"Good flight babe?" I asked nervously.

"No actually, fucking shit to put it mildly" replied Lakey.

"Well, while you were in Hong Kong Muskrat had a few people over, a couple of drinks were spilled and the carpet got a bit damaged when he was doing the splits during a drinking game" I coughed out, adding to her almighty furious mood. Lakey looked fit to explode and rightly so, her face turned purple; and then it all came out.

"I've been in Hong Kong hearing all about you" she screamed. For the next five minutes she went on to explain, down to the smallest detail, about Tara and what had been said to her on the trip, times, places, the whole nine yards. As she finished, in a rage she picked up the iron, which was still plugged in, and launched it at me. As I ducked down, the hot steel projectile hit the wall and stuck into the plasterboard and began smouldering. Lakey burst into tears and thundered upstairs. Fuck! What a nightmare! It was my fault and I knew it.

Refusing to come out from the bedroom, I left for my flight knowing that I had upset someone really special to me and for what? A bit of rough and tumble; what a dickhead. I phoned her several times before my flight and also text her to say sorry and that I loved her. Once in Miami, I tried to call her continuously but she was not responding.

Once back in the UK, she and I had a lot of sorting out to do. In a relationship, once someone has lost trust it's usually over and finished. I tried everything in the book to sort this out but nothing was happening or working. Lakey moved to her mum's for a bit to try and get her head sorted out, she was a good person and I had fucked it up. I left her to have some space and hoped she would come around but she was wounded, and eventually came to the decision that it was over and that we would have to sell the house and move out. Shit!

CHAPTER 23

AIR RAGE

Certain things happen in your life that can change the direction in which it is heading; some good and some not so good. Mistakes dictate your future destiny and I was about to enter a new phase in my life but if I could have turned back the clock on the previous episode, I would have done so, absolutely.

Life moves in mysterious ways and as fate would have it my parents were moving from the North of England to Marlow-on-Thames in Buckinghamshire. My Dad had got a new job and the company was transferring him with a relocation buy-out, which was a terrific result, as they had to buy him a house in Marlow (one of the most affluent, amazing places in the UK) to a similar standard as their place up in the North East. Since I had just sold my house and made a load of money on it, I bought my parents place in Newcastle. Timing is a funny thing in life.

Their new house was wonderful and only twenty minutes from Heathrow on a good day, which was ideal for me if I ever had an early check-in or arrived back late on a flight. It meant living back in the North East, which I loved and would have to commute down on British Midland or British Airways, but I didn't mind that as you only had to do it once a week; I had the best of both worlds really.

At this point I had to reflect on my flying career and see if it was what I really wanted to do. As it turned out I was eligible to apply for Purser now, which most people thought was hilarious and I would have no chance in succeeding. Muskrat was in the same boat and we decided to give it a go. With the applications sent off, Muskrat and I were off to Washington on a rostered flight together.

Now Washington was my least favourite destination we flew to; an early afternoon arrival, early check-out. Although the Hotel was very nice, it was downtown in the Washington D.C. business district, not a lot to do there, no shopping malls nearby etc; once you had visited the White House and the War Memorials you had, more or less, seen the lot.

On board the flight to Washington our application for promotion to Purser was the topic of conversation. Everyone seemed to have an opinion but the general consensus was; we had no chance, we were just too wild, and not the yes sir, no sir people they wanted to promote. Jeremy, the camp Purser from economy was particularly vocal in his opinion of our pending promotions. Now the camp guys are good at their job on board, particularly customer service and attention to detail. However,

should things go particularly pear-shaped, i.e. air rage, they are useless. Muskrat pointed this out to him and he skipped out of the galley and back to his duties; in other words fuck off. We were starting to get depressed at everyone putting us down. After all, we were a couple of good fun characters and we would be good for crew moral if we were in charge.

Once at the hotel in Washington Muskrat and I could concentrate on our project that we had to do for our Purser interview. It was decided that we had to produce a tourist-style brochure to present to the interview panel concerning the new destination launch to Barbados, what is to see and do there as well as the do's and don'ts etc.

The good thing about the business hotel in Washington was all the internet facilities available. We could use them for free to help us prepare our projects.

We spent several hours brain-storming ideas off each other and maximised our time there to the full. Little did we know that the return flight we were about to board would change our career paths forever!

The flight back Saturday afternoon was pretty light, barely half-full, which was a plus as it would be a nice easy sector. When you have a full load on board, you have very little chance of getting any rest; but half-full, like we were today, the In-flight Supervisor had decided that we could have one and a half hours each. With the services out of the way, Muskrat and I made our way downstairs to the familiar bunks on the A-340 Airbus; lights out, it was time for a nice, relaxing snooze.

As I drifted into a deep sleep, I was woken suddenly by the thunder of footsteps coming down the stairs.

"Quick you two, get dressed and get upstairs, we've got real problems with a passenger who has gone berserk" said Jill, the Purser.

We hurriedly dressed and headed up to the forward galley to find out what was going on. As it turned out a passenger from economy had lost the plot, had been drinking his own spirit combined with medication and lashing out at one of the crew, had broken her nose. We observed Hayley, the young air-hostess, as an ice compress and bandage were being applied to her face.

The bastard! My blood was boiling.

Jill went on to explain the problem: this guy, who had lost the plot, was huge and a well nasty piece of work. As Muskrat and I headed down to the back of the plane, we could hear him before we saw him. Sure enough he was massive, tattoos everywhere, thick muscular arms, he reminded you of someone who had spent all his life on a building site. A rugged skin face, square jaw and angry eyes greeted us as we approached him. Because he was so menacing all the passengers around him were not at all keen to get involved and who could blame them? Jeremy, the economy gay Purser, had legged it as well (there's a shock!!), so it was down to Muskrat and myself.

Being from Newcastle, I'd seen more than the odd scuffle in my life so I felt pretty calm and confident as I approached this angry individual. Having Muskrat as back up was a bonus and being a rugby player from Wales added to my confidence.

"So what's the problem mate? Someone upset you?" I asked in my calm Geordie accent,

"Fuck off, you northern monkey" he screamed back at me. Hmmm! maybe another line of questioning might help.

"Look, you shouting like that is scaring everyone. You've hurt one of the young girls, let's calm down and

165

talk to me, what's going on?" I said to him more firmly this time.

He put his hands over his face and began to rock backwards and forwards in his seat. Jesus, we had real problems here; I pointed to Muskrat the near empty bottle of brandy that was by his seat. Okay, let's think. I realised our best chance was to get him into the galley which was only a couple of rows from where he was sitting. After about fifteen minutes of negotiating we managed to coax him in there. Phew! Excellent! If it all went pear-shaped now and we had to resort to Kung Fu at least it would be out of sight of the passengers.

I'd managed to establish that his name was Tom, but very little else. Out of his sight, a couple of crew had prepared the restraint kit in case we needed it (handcuffs etc).

"So Tom, are you married or single?" I asked him,

"Women, I fucking hate women" he replied angrily.

As I was thinking of another question, Tom put his arm around my back, in a kind of friendly way.

"You're alright Geordie man, it's all those other wankers" he said, shaking.

With his arm around my neck, he eased me into a semi-headlock and I don't think he realised his own strength as I began to turn blue. Muskrat realised the situation and kicked Tom's legs away, decking him to the ground. As I released myself from his grip an almighty scuffle ensued with arms and legs everywhere. A really violent struggle!

We eventually managed to get three large American passengers to help us and they sat on him while we applied the restraints and handcuffs, all the while still spitting and struggling, trying to lash out, he was so strong. Eventually, when he realised the game was over, he relented and calmly asked for a fag.

The galley floor was covered in blood and looked like a war zone, blankets had been placed down around "Mad Tom", as he was now known, and with our lunatic restrained we headed up front for a sit down. Totally exhausted, I collapsed into the nice, big, upper-class seat. My shirt was ripped and covered in blood, God knows what would have happened had the Muskrat and I not been on the flight.

On landing the police boarded the plane and Tom was escorted off to a thunderous applause from everyone on board. It was a major incident and made the national press. We received letters of thanks from loads of people including the airline and our Line Managers, who phoned to thank us for our efforts. This was just the incident that could swing our Purser interviews and promotions. Well, I was sure it wouldn't do us any harm anyway.

CHAPTER 24

"YOO PLAYS GOLF BETTER ZAN YOO MAKES LOVE!"

Our interview day was upon us and, before we had time to breathe the moment had arrived. A member of the Pink Mafia, a Line Manager and a Human Resources representative would be interviewing all the potential candidates. Fully uniformed and a little nervous I entered the interview room. The Pink Mafia representative was of a lower ranking status than normal, which could work in my favour. I knew the Line Manager quite well and got on with her so I might just have a chance here, I said to myself. As it turned out, all they were really interested in was the air rage incident that I had recently been involved in. I spent the entire interview going through, in minute detail, the whole episode (it had been a huge success and the airline had come out of it with a glowing reputation). A quick three minute presentation at the end about

Barbados and I was out of there. Muskrat's interview was more or less identical,

"Well Muskrat, if we don't get the job now, with everything in our favour, we never will" I said as we left the Virgin Head Offices.

Sure enough, a week later we received our letters to advise us of our successful promotions. Happy days and a new episode in my life was about to begin.

The course was completed and a week of brain-washing out of the way, my first official flight as a Purser was to Boston, a place I really liked. The hotel we stayed in was wonderful, it was a Golf and Country Club and had a fantastic championship golf course attached to it. I was going to take full advantage of this; as it was late September it would probably be the last chance to play before snow and bad weather arrived and the course would be closed for five months.

The In-flight Supervisor for the flight was one psycho-host beast from hell," Janet scary-eyes Lowes". Now this woman would make Myra Hindley look tame. Really scary, this lady! She was training, part time, to be a psychology counsellor. Christ, her first patient should be herself. Talk about putting the crew on edge with her scary eye activity. I decided to work in economy down the back and be as far away from scary Janet as possible.

Working as Purser I found very rewarding and was determined not to be the tyrant, dictator-style boss that was all too common and for all the wrong reasons. My theory on the job was to give the crew a really nice, comfortable working environment and to trouble-shoot around any problems that might occur. The flight itself was pretty smooth and Janet kept herself out of my way, thank God. The only problem I had was when a passenger said they had ordered a lacto vegetarian, instead of a normal vegetarian meal. No problem, just get the magic felt tip pen out and write on the tin foil "lacto", problem solved and see you in Boston; what the eye doesn't see the heart doesn't feel etc.

With the flight out of the way and upon arriving at the hotel, I got chatting to the hotel manager to see if he could fix me up with a game of golf. Over the years I had got to know him pretty well and that familiarity networking relationship stood me in good stead, should I ever need a favour. Sure enough he phoned my room to confirm the tee-off time as nine am the following morning, excellent! With that taken care of I headed to the bar to see if there were any potential casualties on the Serengeti plains.

All of the juniors from economy, who I had been looking after, made it down to the bar along with the flight deck, but all the guys from the front had opted out (I think that Janet had traumatised them all as usual). We ordered a few snacks and the drinks were sent over, everyone had to produce identification as proof they were twenty one, which made me laugh as the Captain was sixty and looked older! But that's America for you, everything to extremes, you can buy a gun at twenty one but unless you have I.D you can't get a drink; even if you look sixty five and are from England.

If I thought that it was easy to pull being a senior, then being Purser was a doddle. On this flight I had the choice of eight, potentially willing candidates but a young lady at the opposite end of the bar had caught my attention. She was part of the German Lufthansa crew that shared the hotel and was absolutely stunning. The usual after flight activities were in full flow, plenty of drink, lots of eye contact and flirting, the flight deck boring everyone with stories about aircraft and leaf blowers that they were going to buy.

The girl from Lufthansa had been giving me plenty of looks, so I decided to be brave and ask her to join us for a game of pool. The Virgin girls weren't too keen on the two Germans who had joined us, but I just fancied a bit of "Vorsprung durch Technik".

By now I was in full flow and my spiel, including a couple of references to Faulty Tower's famous German episode as well as Uncle Albert's (from Only Fools and Horses) interrogation of a young, pregnant German girl in the Nags Head, was going down a storm.

I was making massive progress! I had established that her name was Ellen; she was twenty seven years old and had been airline crew for five years. She loved to play golf and agreed to join me for a game the following morning. After a few games of pool the crew made their excuses and drifted off and I was left with Ellen, laughing and talking about nothing in particular. Both of us had just experienced difficult flights, so now we just wanted hard sex, I wondered if she had hairy armpits! Hmmm, I hoped not. An invite to my room for a Baileys on ice had been accepted and we were on our way.

No sooner were the drinks poured, the first sips taken and it was down to business. Christ, she wanted it more than me. Ellen was a really aggressive lover, not what I was used to, different and very demanding. After a hard flight and a number of drinks, her vigorous demands were taking their toll and I was in a bit of a selfish mood. As I rolled over and collapsed after sex, I could tell she wanted more but I was done and advised her that we would continue in the morning. Sure enough at first light, Ellen was awake and wanting more sex, God this girl was insatiable. A slightly better performance this time on my part, and it was time for breakfast and golf.

Ellen looked so elegant in her all-in-one, light green, fitted outfit. It fitted her perfectly in all the right places. I couldn't help but congratulate myself on such a terrific result. As ladies go, she was a very good golfer and we enjoyed a great day out. I happened to produce some heroics on the golf course, off my dodgy 6 handicap and could see Ellen was well impressed with my golfing abilities. A little bit of lunch after golf and it was back to my room for a quick rough and tumble before check-out. I was desperate for a sleep so a quick, hard penetration of Ellen, taking her from behind, finished me off. As I collapsed onto the bed, breathing heavily, gazing at the ceiling, I took Ellen's hand and she looked at me with large and very disappointed eyes;

"Gary, I have to tell you something" she said in a pigeon German- English accent,

"Oh yes?" I replied.

"Yoo plays golf better zan yoo makes love" she responded with scowling eyes.

I tried not to laugh but that was it, such a great comment; wait till the lads hear that one!

.

"YOO PLAYS GOLF BETTER ZAN YOO MAKES LOVE"

Down at checkout in the hotel reception, Janet was clucking around like a maniac in her usual, panic-stricken, hurried demeanour that made everyone feel uneasy. What an idiot I thought to myself. After all, stress is failure in coping with pressure. Aidy, one of the seniors, was looking pretty distracted and not his usual self, I had noticed it on the way out, but hadn't had a chance to ask him if all was okay on the outbound sector. The crew-buses pulled up and we handed our suitcases to the driver. Once on board I found Aidy down the back of the bus, staring aimlessly out of the window. Hmmm that's odd! I sat next to him and asked if he was okay as he seemed a bit pre-occupied, he obviously was.

He told me that his Mum had died a few days before this trip and he had decided to fly to keep himself busy and take his mind off everything. Poor bastard! I thought. "Listen Aidy, you know where I am on the flight, if you need a chat come down and see me" I said sympathetically; he nodded gratefully and we headed off to Boston airport.

With the crew flight-safety checks out of the way, all the equipment in the respective areas checked and

174

passed onto Janet, we were ready for boarding. The flight back was only going to be five and a half hours due to the tail wind and with a totally full load it was going to be a hectic flight. The services just flowed into each other, a little bit chaotic but I just about managed to get away with a hassle-free sector.

Pleased with my efforts down the back in economy and with about forty-five minutes to land I headed to the front to give Janet my paperwork for landing. As I approached her double jump seat at the forward door of the aircraft, she was deep in conversation with the upper-class Purser about Aidy, that he was useless and incompetent at the job and had done a scathing assessment on him. Mortified on hearing their verbal attack I had to intervene.

"Listen ladies, do you know why Aidy is probably not at his best today?" I asked in a serious tone of voice.

"Well he's a straight guy isn't he? And you're all lazy" replied Janet in her Essex twang.

"Listen you tunnel-vision idiot, Aidy's Mum just died and he came to work as he thought it might help him take his mind off the problem you know, like you do when something awful like that happens in your life" I snapped at her.

"ERR Oh yeah really?" she replied,

"Yeah: Really! Didn't it occur to you to ask the lad if he was okay, you self-centred bitch, you're supposed to be a trained counsellor and that's fucking out of order" I fired back.

"Well he should have told me" she answered nervously.

"Told you; Bollocks! If I hadn't walked in and heard your conversation just now he would have been handed an assessment on top of everything else that has happened to him, and just because you couldn't ask him if he was okay, you just assumed that because he is a straight guy. You should be ashamed, it's a total disgrace!" I shouted.

I then handed her my paperwork and walked off. Our conversation had been overheard by a few people including cabin crew but I didn't care, it had to be said and I was right. Aidy phoned me after we landed to thank me for speaking up for him.

Janet was so wrong and such an uncaring person. I don't think anyone had ever shouted at her like that before, but it had to be said. I knew that she was good friends with The Crow and the Pink Mafia people; that this incident would be discussed over and over again and I reckoned my card was marked.

CHAPTER 25

ROAD RAGE, AIR RAGE......
NOW GOLF RAGE!

With my first Purser flight out of the way I headed to my parents place in Marlow for relaxation and a chill-out. They had a beautiful place in Weatherhead Park, two minutes from the River Thames, and as the weather was wonderful at the time, there wasn't a better place to be. Since I had five days off work I decided to head up to the North East the following evening. I caught the last British Midland flight from Heathrow to Teesside. I had got to know the British Midland girls pretty well now and in particular a lovely, young airhostess called Lisa. Woody had a bit of previous with her but had moved on now and rumour had it he had fallen in love with a Virgin beauty from York.

Sure enough, Lisa was on the flight and she greeted me with a big smile and a kiss on the cheek. She had been flying all day, back and forth from Teesside to

Heathrow and this was her last sector for the day. I advised her that what she needed after a hard days work was a nice glass of wine back at my place.

"Oh why not?" she replied in a joyful manner.

What a lifestyle I had, flying all over the world, pulling birds for fun, would I ever get fed-up with this? I couldn't see it and here I am, off to my place with a beautiful airhostess from the airline I commute on. God is smiling at me at the moment and long may it continue.

Back at my pad with the wine poured and the flirting banter going down a storm, it was time for action. I don't know what it is about a woman in uniform, it's just so appealing and with the bottle of wine nearly empty it was time to make love. Lifting her skirt up high and removing her white G-string, we made the most passionate love, right there on the sofa, very naughty and most appealing.

I love the North East so much, people are much friendlier and characters like Janet Lowes don't exist. The following day I said goodbye to Lisa and headed off to the golf course for some therapeutic, down to earth, piss-taking banter. I'd arranged to play with Ginger Philly Dog and Brian 'they never made it to the moon' Hirst. Now Philly Dog is the most angry, aggressive golfer that has ever lived, if he hits a bad shot, his face goes purple and then he turns into the Incredible Hulk and launches his club helicopter fashion down the fairway. Great fun to watch and it helped me de-stress. On one occasion when I was playing with him, upon missing a putt from six inches, he took hold of his putter and launched it out of the course and into a farmer's corn field, the corn being about four feet high. After calming him down, he felt guilty and regretted his actions. But he couldn't find his expensive putter anywhere in the field. In the end he borrowed a metal detector from someone to locate it, but all he found was a horse shoe and the putter has not been seen since. The good thing about escaping the airline environment was that you could totally unwind, away from some of the idiots with whom you had to fly. I explained to Philly Dog and Brian about my last flight and what went on, both of them were amazed and dumfounded as to how one didn't end up whacking someone.

CHAPTER 26

MILLENNIUM FEVER........
AND THE BIG BLACK THING!!

At this time all the airline gossip was about the millennium and where you would be flying to, would the aircraft be able to fly, would air-traffic computers just crash the system and the world would be in total chaos? All the usual scaremongering nonsense that was exaggerated beyond belief within the airline circles. As we eagerly awaited our rosters to advise us of our millennium destinations, I was over the moon when I found out I was going to Chicago, Woody had been rostered for the trip as well, so it should be a flight to remember.

It had grabbed everyone, millennium fever was here. Woody and I were off to Chicago and it would be a trip to remember, that's for sure. The atmosphere on board the flight was amazing. The crew were wicked, from the Captain down to the most junior crew. The Captain had his wife with him and the crew in the majority had brought a friend along for company and the experience. After all, in years to come you will always remember where you were when the millennium arrived.

Everyone was in a party mood including all the passengers and even the Americans. On arriving at our wonderful hotel in downtown Chicago, the Management had pulled out all the stops to make sure everyone had a brilliant time. All the rooms had been upgraded and the Hotel Manager had provided us with our own suite on the Penthouse floor so we could hold a private millennium party. Once we returned from the firework display that was held at the edge of the lake (starting at eleven thirty) I will never forget that New Years Eve night.

Everyone was suited and booted, fully glammed up and ready to party. We met at the Penthouse suite at five thirty pm, firstly to celebrate the New Year in London since we were six hours behind in Chicago. As the clock of Big Ben ticked down on the giant TV screen in the centre of the room, the whole place erupted and champagne corks and party whistles echoed around the place in a crescendo; lots of kissing, shaking hands and clinking of glasses followed.

As the party got into full swing, (it was another six hours before the Americans' turn), it was time to get stuck into all the free drink that had been laid on for us and very welcome it was. With the room packed full of airline crew and their companions, it was interesting to watch the party atmosphere of everyone in such a buoyant mood. One of the girls on the trip, Julie, had previously had a rough and tumble with me on a few occasions so I knew I was okay for a bit of fun that night. With the pressure off to pull it was time to relax and get drunk.

Woody, who was now totally in love with Claire from York, was attracting attention from several of the young girls and their companions, but he was making it known to everyone he was not interested. What a turnaround? He changed from being Fred West to a choirboy in two months. At around eleven thirty, we headed down to the lakeside to watch the firework display. Since it was minus seven outside, everyone was wrapped up with big coats, scarves and hats. The firework display was incredible! It must have cost millions of dollars. As we all kissed and hugged each other again as midnight arrived, one of the girls was particularly keen to give Woody a tongue swapping session, but he was only happy for a peck on the lips or a smacker on the cheek but definitely no tongues. In the end he had to pull his woolly hat down over his face like someone from the SAS to avoid a tongue being rammed into his mouth. Watching this I found most amusing, I mean that girl was pretty tasty and two months earlier, Woody would readily have accepted this invitation of friendship and tongue tennis, God he really must be in love!

Back at the Penthouse, things were really moving, what a party? We had been joined by a few uninvited strangers, but who cared? Everyone was having a great time. With party hats on and whistles blowing, we were dancing the night away. I'd obtained some black, party spray string along the way and dispensed half the can into the partying crowd. As we took a small break to pour some drinks, I asked Woody if he had seen this spray before. It's well powerful! To demonstrate what I meant I aimed it at the wall and drew a big, eight foot penis including testicles, onto the white wall. The huge black member glared back at us and we roared with laughter and then continued to party. I finally called it a night at 6.00am and headed off to my room with Julie to let the New Year in. I was in a bit of a daze and dived onto the bed ready for the Millennium shag. Happy days!!!

"First one of the New Year" I remembered saying when we had finished.

It had been arranged that at eleven am I would meet Woody in his room for a Millennium New Year's day breakfast and champagne. I said goodbye to Julie and headed to Woody's room. I knocked on his door and he let me in, wearing a tiny towel around his waist. (As usual)

He looked a little pensive and preoccupied as he jumped back into bed, sitting bolt upright with his back against the headboard. I poured the champagne.

"Are you alright son?" I asked, wondering at his demeanour.

"Well Gazza, I've got something to tell you, it's very important" Woody replied thoughtfully.

Oh shit! He's going to tell me he's bent. I nervously backed towards the wall, keeping my arse away from his view. Jesus, Woody a homo? I thought; leather trousers, handle-bar moustache, ouch!

"Well, its Claire, you see I'm totally in love and I'm going to ask her to marry me" Woody said, smiling like a Cheshire cat. Fuck! I can't tell you how relieved I was to hear that, married and not gay, how brilliant! We chinked our champagne glasses and I congratulated him on his news and hoped the year 2000 was going to be a great year for us. At that point the phone rang and it was Claire, she was in Miami for her trip and was obviously missing Woody big time. For the next twenty minutes it was

"No, I love you more"

"No, I love you more"

"No, you hang up first". It was like being in a Mills and Boon novel. Finally the credit on her phone card expired and it was over.

After breakfast we talked about what the forthcoming New Year would bring and Woody asked me to be his Best Man, wow, what a start to the year. The phone rang again, God not Claire again I thought. Woody answered it and it was for me, it was Jamie Davies the In-flight Supervisor.

"Gazza, we've got big problems. Someone has drawn an eight foot penis in black spray on the wall last night and it won't come off" said Jamie in a panic-stricken voice.

"Oh dear" I replied.

"Well we need to advise the Hotel Manager, can you come down and help me out with an explanation?" he asked.

"Sure I can" I answered, feeling rather guilty.

I told Woody about the conversation and he rolled onto the bed and howled, belly laughing,

"I can't wait to see the Manager's face when he sees that" said Woody, chuckling.

Down at reception I met Jamie and we asked to see the Hotel Manager. As he approached, the butterflies kicked in

"Happy New Year gentlemen, how can I help you today?" he said smiling and happy. Jamie nudged me to speak,

"Well, we had a party last night in one of the suites as you know, and well, er, something got sprayed onto the wall and it won't come off" I said apprehensively.

"Okay, never mind. What is it? These things do happen, especially at the millennium" he replied, still in a cheerful tone,

"Well I think you'd better come and see for yourself sir" said Jamie (not having the heart to tell him that it was an eight foot penis),

"Sure! No problem. Let's go!" replied the Manager. Once into the lift we headed up to the Penthouse floor. I looked at Jamie in a kind of dreaded "Oh shit!" facial expression and he returned the same regard.

"So how are the BEARS doing this year?" I asked referring to the Chicago Bears American football team.

"Great" replied the Manager. I was just trying to get on his good side before he witnessed a shocking sight. Jamie raised his eyebrows and I shrugged my shoulders back at him. We opened the Penthouse Suite and invited him in.

"Well sir, this is what will not come off the wall, it's stuck like tar, must have reacted with the paint or something" I said in a soft voice.

As he looked at the wall, the colour drained from his face and his lips began to blubber.

"Jesus Christ! Well, who? What? ......how did it happen?" he demanded, almost lost for words as he stared, mortified, at the huge member.

"Don't know, we had a few gate-crashers last night, maybe one of them did it. Look, we're really sorry but we don't know who did it and we wanted to bring it to your attention" I said hoping for a bit of sympathy

We left the plush suite and headed off down to his office. Luckily he took the incident well and asked us to have a whip around all our group to get some money together that could be used as a tip for the poor guy who was going to be called in on New Years Day to repair the damage. After all, the room couldn't be used until the thing had been removed.

Jamie knew that I had something to do with it but I was denying everything. Once you admit to something in Virgin, that's it, disciplinary, no questions asked, so the best policy, unless they had video evidence or five eye witnesses, deny everything Baldric. With two hundred and fifty dollars collected and handed to the Manager, he was happy with our efforts and finally saw the funny side of it and probably tells that story to everyone today.

On the flight back home Woody's words had got me thinking. You know, maybe I should settle down a bit, maybe this was the year when I should do it. Yeah! Right!

CHAPTER 27

A NAUGHTY BOY

With the millennium out of the way it was time for a few good trips to start off the New Year, Barbados and Antigua were proving to be good venues, and in particular a five night Antigua was most welcome to top up the tan in the winter. I had requested a skiing trip to LAX with Barry "The Silver Fox" and a few other lads who had been flying about six months, nicked-named the "Venga Boys". A really good bunch who had all trained together and reminded me of how Muskrat and I were when we first started, up for everything and mad for it.

The theme for their trip was the seventies. Everyone who was working in economy had to wear flower power shirts and big curly wigs and glasses, great fun and the passengers loved it. The bottom line was, as long as the passengers were getting well looked after and they were happy with the service it didn't matter if the crew was having fun and enjoying themselves. That's something that the psycho-host beasts and Pink Mafia failed to realise.

Barry, "The Silver Fox" was a star, a real top bloke. Branson had wanted to promote him further up the ladder on a number of occasions, but Barry was content with his life and the days off this lifestyle provided for him. One of the big problems the airline had was that the right people just didn't want to be promoted. So generally, far less capable applicants would get the job, especially cabin-crew officer based positions.

I remembered when I first started and two positions for Line Manager and Trainer came up. Only two people applied for the positions, one of them being The Crow, so they had to give her the job as they were desperate.

The flight to LAX was a blast and the ten hour sector flew by. Into the hotel in Marina Del Ray, I was greeted by the familiar sight and sound of the head receptionist Gi-Gi, a tiny lady from Scotland, who dismayed at some of the cabin-crews antics. She once said that Virgin crew would wreck Buckingham Palace if they ever stayed there.

"Hello Gary May you naughty little boy" said Gi-Gi as I gathered my key and money from reception,

"Hiya Gi-Gi you old slapper" I replied, rather cheekily.

"Oh, you're cheeky, you are Gary May, I hope that you're going to behave yourself this time, I'm keeping my eye on you" Gi-Gi continued in her fabulous squeaky, Scottish, accent.

"No chance of that Gi-Gi, I'm with the Venga boys and The Silver Fox and we're up for a mad one" I answered, laughing as Gi-Gi caught a glimpse of this mad bunch as they filed into the hotel.

"Oh my God, we had better get extra security in" she remarked.

The first night in the bar, all the usual arrival antics were going on, the Venga Boys were all trying to out do each other to try and impress the ladies. The Silver Fox and I just took a back seat; we'd seen it all before and had bought the t-shirt. Tomorrow was going to be a wicked day of snowboarding up at Big Bear and as we had a really early departure ahead of us, I was taking it easy. Leaving the Venga Boys to it like kids in a playground, we called it a night to get ready for the trip.

At five am the three crew buses pulled into the reception ready for departure. Coffee and doughnuts in hand it was time to show the Venga Boys and other crew a wicked trip up the mountain. Having done the journey up there so many times before, I knew the route like the back of my hand. A few of the crew were a bit worse for wear from the previous night's drinking but the fresh, clean, mountain air would soon remedy that. Getting all the crew kitted out, I felt like a parent looking after their children, offering advice and guidance.

We couldn't have picked a better day. With fresh powder snow and beautiful, crystal clear, cloud free sky, you had to pinch yourself as it appeared to be a dream. It's hard to believe that you're only two and a half hours drive away from the hustle and bustle of Los Angles City; it really was a precious jewel of a place. The Venga Boys and the rest of the crew had a fantastic day. For most of them it was their first time on skis and snowboards, so the new experience for them was wicked. Watching them all learning and having wipe-outs was hilarious. I think I spent most of the day in the beginners' area with the Silver Fox, enjoying the carnage and colourful language emitted by the crew having such a good time. This is what the airline job was all about, a bunch of fun loving, like minded individuals enjoying life to the full. At the end of a long day it was back to LAX and Marina Del Ray to reflect on a fantastic outing. Everyone thanked us for taking them up there and introducing winter sports to their portfolios of life's experiences.

Back at the hotel Gi-Gi greeted us with her usual cutting, Scottish wit.

"I hope you're not going to be too noisy tonight Gary May, you naughty boy" she said. It was time for a quick shower then into the bar to discuss all the wipe-outs and fun happenings of the day. The atmosphere in the bar after a day out skiing and snowboarding was brilliant, frantic chatter and laughter echoed around the room. With healthy, glowing, sun-kissed skin the feel good factor was at a premium. I hadn't even considered trying to pull anyone so far on the trip and was just enjoying the fun banter and piss-taking. I was oblivious to a certain young lady who was interested in me until Gemma, one of the girls, advised me that a tall, long legged brunette had got the hots for me and I only had to say the word and I was in. Happy days!! The lady in question, Colleen, had been on the Venga Boys training course and was good friends with them but not in a sexual way. She thought they were all a bit young and daft. I hadn't really chatted to her that much during the days skiing, only to help her stand up a couple of times and I was really pleased to hear this good news. I sat with Gemma and Colleen for a while and laughed and joked about our day out, she was tremendous, a perfect figure, long legs, straight brown hair and a model face, she was also a really down to earth girl and very easy to talk to. If I played my cards right this could be a good result. The trick now was timing, how to get Colleen and myself out of the bar without attracting anyone's attention and up to my room for some more winter sports activities. Being an expert now in the art of pulling in LAX, I waited till Colleen had to go to the toilet and timed it so we would meet as she came back out. Sure enough, years of training bore fruit and we met face to face outside the toilet, out of sight of the bar.

"Hi Colleen; what a day; I don't know about you but I'm about ready to call it a night" I said hinting and hoping at the same time

"Yes me too, it's been fabulous though hasn't it?" she replied, smiling with naughty, glinting eyes.

"Look, why don't we go and have a drink in my room and a bit of a chat, Miss long legs?" I answered.

"Yeah great, absolutely, why not?" she said seductively. I took her hand, we kissed passionately and I could feel really good chemistry.

"Let's leg it before anyone sees us" I said to her, and we were gone.

A perfectly executed escape I have to say and no-one saw anything. Great! As we headed past reception Gi-Gi caught a glimpse of Colleen and I as the lift opened, "Gary May you're a very naughty boy, watch him Miss, he's too cheeky for his own good" said Gi-Gi.

. "Good night Gi-Gi you old banger" I replied. Phew! Luckily the lift the doors closed and we were away. We had practically undressed each other before we got to my room. What a fantastic figure and to cap it all, she had the most fantastic landing strip, trimmed to perfection, almost with military precision and she had also had a boob enlargement which was very pleasing to the eye; any good? For the next fourteen hours, we never got out of bed, what a fantastic time. You know what? I might just start seeing Colleen for a bit; she's a top girl and they don't come along very often I said to myself.

Sure enough the Venga Boys were all gutted when they found out about Colleen and me. I think they had all fallen in love with her during their training course, but it was I who had walked away with the prize! Well done the Gazza! Colleen and I saw each other for a couple of months afterwards, and spent loads of time at my parents place in Marlow and up in Newcastle. She was a Southend girl at heart and I think the madness and forwardness of the Newcastle girls scared her off ever wanting to move up there. In the end we decided to call it a day, we both wanted different things at that stage of our lives and Colleen didn't want to settle as she was only twenty three. Fair enough and, since we had both organised separate summer holidays, we agreed to stay friends with no animosity at all.

I was off to Ibiza for the full Ibiza experience.

CHAPTER 28

IBIZA FEVER.......
AND DONT FEED THE HORSE!

A trip to Ibiza had been organised for ten mad airline personnel to experience the full fruits of life. It was organised primarily so everybody could try anything they wanted in a totally liberated way. A good friend of the Muskrat by the name of Horse (for obvious reasons), also a Hugh Grant look-alike, had booked our party villa on the internet and what a place it was. Another friend of Muskrat's, Adams, was in charge of chemicals and joint rolling. He had a particular knack of being able to roll the perfect joint, a very important member of the team on this trip.

On arriving early Sunday morning, we picked up the two hire cars and headed for the villa. Horse had done us proud and the villa he had chosen was magnificent. It was an old Spanish style house in its own grounds, surrounded by vineyards and olive groves. It nestled in a valley outside the small village of Jesus, looking down onto Ibiza town. What a place, pure luxury! A kidney-shaped, sunken pool surrounded by five hammocks strung up into the trees, two circular hot-tub Jacuzzis were at each end of the pool and bubbling away under the morning sun.

"Well Horse, well done mate, you couldn't have done any better here" I said and patted him on the back. After unpacking and checking out the rooms, it was time for the fun to begin.

Adams and Scottish James headed into San Antonio to collect the necessary chemicals and the rest of us grabbed the sun beds and hit the pool. Muskrat, who was in charge of the music, cranked up the ghetto blaster and hard-house tunes blared, echoing down the valley. Great fun! After about four hours of bang, bang, thud, thud music, I asked him for a change of tunes.

"You got any Simply Red son?" I asked, head thumping by now.

"Bollocks!! That music is for homos! No Simply Red and pussy stuff on this trip son, its danger music all the way" replied Muskrat who was backed up by the rest of the gang.

A beautiful sunset back-dropped the sky and it was time for our first night out. Clubbing gear ironed, hair gelled to the maximum and we were all ready. I had recently been hitting the gym heavily and had got myself into pretty good shape, not quite a six-pack, more like a four-pack, but I felt good. I had taken Woody's advice and had my chest waxed for the trip (ouch!), smooth as a babies bum.

"Right lets go into San Antonio" I shouted and we were off.

We took in a couple of bars in the west end, topping up with Budweiser and Sambucca shots along the way. Then we were off to Eden to see Judge Jules, a kind of medium strength DJ who normally put on a good show and got the crowd going.

As we walked along the sea front near the Egg, Jamsie handed me a tablet.

"There you go son, your first disco biscuit". Slightly reluctantly and nervously I swallowed the pill identified with a strange logo (I had heard all the stories about E-tablets and what can happen, but I took the plunge never the less).

"You know something lads? I don't know why I'm taking this pill because drugs don't affect me, I'm too strong minded for them" I said confidently.

"Yeah right; you wait and tell me that in about forty-five minutes" replied Jamsie and laughed.

Once into Eden, it was packed, fantastic atmosphere and banging tunes. Jamsie handed me a bottle of water and told me to make sure I drank plenty of it during the night. Up until this trip I was quite happy with a load of beers or Bacardi, do a nice little Phil Collins shuffle on the dance floor and that was me contented. Here I was in a strange environment with banging tunes, flashing strobes and loads of podium dancers going crazy; plus I'd just taken an ecstasy tablet thirty minutes earlier. Muskrat came over and asked if I was okay

"Yeah, very happy, tablet not working though, I knew I was too strong for them" I said disappointedly.

Suddenly a change of beat in the music to a classic dance tune "Darude" and an almighty rush of adrenalin ripped through my veins and into my head. What a rush! I was buzzing. That was it, the next thing I know I'm up on the podium going berserk. Mental! The rest of the lads, on seeing this, are hysterical. Jamsie had to walk away; the sight of me in a totally lost frenzy had made him laugh so hard his ribs were nearly caving in. I was on one now, what a feeling! Buzzing and flying out of control. Muskrat looked up at me on the podium, smiling like a Cheshire cat

"Gazza, Phil Collins is dead, go on the Big Fella" he shouted and shook his head in disbelief. I felt like I was on cloud nine, scantily clad babes everywhere, this was amazing. Feeling like the most confident bloke in the world I chatted and rubbed myself against hardened female clubbers, telling them I was what they wanted and let's go back to the villa for a private party.

At some point during the night I got attached to a young, nineteen year old Norwegian girl who was off her nut as well and I proceeded to try and speak Norwegian to her and somehow I think I just about managed it. I found out her name was Lila and she was in this club with her cousin but didn't know where she was. From Eden we headed off to Playa Den Bossa to another nightspot. Finally, it was early morning and as the sun was coming up, it was time to leave. I asked Lila if she fancied coming back to the villa to smoke a joint and get mellow. Sure enough she was up for it and we arrived at the villa just as the sun was coming up over the valley.

The view was breathtaking, we collapsed into a hammock and Adams handed me one of his special joints.

"Do you know, I think heaven must look like this" I whispered into Lila's ear.

Here I was in a hammock with a beautiful, nineteen year old Norwegian, who had hardly anything on, the sun starting to rise, the view was superb and I was puffing on some of the best herbs known to man.

"God, you are a star, life does not get any better" I said to myself.

For the next four days we partied very hard, visiting all the islands' top nightspots, from Amnesia and Manumission through to Space. We met some fantastic people and word had gone out that we had a magnificent villa and were holding crazy, after club, parties. The day before we left there must have been a hundred people there, what a trip!

I have to say the Ibiza experience was a memorable one, but it wasn't something I would want to do week in week out, moderation is the key to life; so that scene would be ok for me now and again.

Some of the other lads however, had fallen in love with that lifestyle. Diesel **Bob** and Ozzie Waine were hooked. Ibiza had sucked **them** in, good luck!

Returning to the UK, it **was** back to reality. Branson was throwing a party in Oxfordshire in the grounds of his house. Fair play to him, all his employees had been invited and you could bring a tent and stay overnight. Everything there was free, from the food and drinks to all the fairground rides, the lot. It was brilliant and looked like the biggest circus in the world had turned up. A group of us headed down there and it was a chance to catch up with a few familiar faces, ex rough and tumbles and share my recent exploits stories about Ibiza. There were literally thousands of people present and loads of ex's milling about all over the place.

I hooked up with Dougie Love, "The Housewives Favourite", and we exchanged stories of our recent conquests and mischief. Time was flying by and it was nearly dark by now, I had been chatting so much that I had lost track of where I was. A huge bonfire had been lit and a large crowd had gathered around it. "The Housewives Favourite", Dougie, was chatting to a couple of girls, Sally and Emily, the latter was someone with whom I had had a previous encounter a couple of months earlier. She was from Blackburn, a good looking girl and loved the London clubbing scene. I told her about my exploits in Ibiza and laughed and chatted to her for ages.

As I had already had a rough and tumble with her I knew I was in for round two, "ding, ding". Dougie had disappeared to his tent with Sally and told me not to disturb him. By now the fire had lost its power and the flames had all but gone so I guided Emily to the tent which Dougie and Sally were occupying.

As we sneaked in, they were both getting down to it. I gave him the thumbs-up as he lay flat on his back, Sally on all fours, giving him a very satisfying blow job. As Emily moved into a similar position and I adjusted myself to get comfortable, she began unzipping my jeans and was eager to start performing, this was lovely. As I turned to observe the goings on between Dougie and Sally, she was now going for it big style and her small, pert bum was only inches away from me. I just couldn't resist it and as it hung in the air, I slid my hand into the erogenous areas, feeding the horse. Unfortunately, Sally got the shock of her life and rose up like a salmon, nearly sticking her head out of the tent. Dougie gasped and wondered what had happened, we both laughed out loud and Dougie decided to move into another tent as Sally wanted total privacy and was a little unhappy with my unexpected, feeding of the horse activity.

The following day, looking like a scene from a Woodstock concert, everyone packed and headed for home. Most people were flying. I was one of the lucky ones who was off for the day, but I did have an early nine o'clock standby duty the following morning, so I decided to stay at my parents that evening in case I got called out. Sure enough at 9.00am the phone rang, that could be only one person, Virgin crewing calling me out on standby, the bastards!

CHAPTER 29

GOLF CAN BE ....
A PAIN IN THE ARSE!

They informed me that I was off to Orlando, one of the hardest flights you had to do at the time. They were always packed to the rafters, hundreds of kids, the passengers had all paid full money for their tickets and their expectations were very high. A nine hour flight normally took its' toll on the crew and you were sometimes lucky to get three people down to the bar afterwards; ah well you had to take the rough with the smooth I thought.

I headed down to Gatwick as quickly as I could, which was a bit of a nightmare travelling along the M25 and M23 on a Monday morning and I made it just within my two and a half hour call-out time. On arriving at the crew check-in, I was advised I was working as In-flight Supervisor since I was the most senior Purser and the assigned Supervisor had posted

203

sick. Not a problem, I had done it before and found the job a doddle.

When flying long haul, the higher up the ladder you go, the less you have to do physically. It's just a case of trouble-shooting, common sense and strategic delegation.

God knows why some of those psycho-host beasts made such hard work for themselves. I'd learnt a lot from The Silver Fox and how he did the job. So I picked up his general strategy and adopted it into my portfolio of working, adding a couple of my own bits along with my gregarious personality.

My professional, upbeat briefing out of the way, we were off to Orlando. The flight there was generally good fun, and you could get away with a lot more than you can on some of the strictly business routes. Competitions for the kids and adults were organised, flight deck visits etc.

The flight was a busy nine hours, no chance of any major crew rest breaks but being in charge on the flight was good. Giving all the crew a nice, chilled-out working environment went a long way to help pass the time

Orlando airport though is a bit of a shambles. When you arrive you get onto trams, find your suitcase once, hand it again, followed by miles of walkways and then try and find your suitcase again, it's a bit of a nightmare really.

Luckily the hotel was spot on and only fifteen minutes from the airport. Around the location are some of the finest golf courses in the world and I had decided to go and play the following morning. Going into Orlando at that time were three flights, two from Gatwick and one from Manchester. The Manchester Crew certainly kept themselves to themselves, but the two Gatwick crews intermingled depending on who you knew. I managed to sort out a game of golf on a magnificent course about twenty minutes drive from the hotel. That taken care of it was time to hit the bar.

A really good turn out from my flight had come down to enjoy a few beers and some unwinding chat. The other two crews did not perform quite as well, probably due to the psycho-host beasts traumatising them all during the flight. Although there were a number of ladies in the bar, nothing had really caught my eye, so I opted for an early night to be fresh for golf the following day.

Golf clubs packed; a quick nip into Denny's for breakfast and it was off to the golf course. After checking in and paying for my green fee, the golf pro advised me that because I was on my own I had been paired with a couple of yanks, Lance and Jo. He smiled as he informed me about this, which made me feel a little suspicious.

On the first tee I warmed up with a couple of practice swings and waited for Lance and Jo to join me. As their golf buggy pulled up I was mortified at the sight before me. Lance was wearing the most horrific pink and yellow golfers' outfit with a matching hat from the 1920's.As it turned out Jo wasn't playing but just along to drive the buggy and assist Lance (Help find his BALLS!).

I introduced myself and Lance skipped over and I shook his camp, loose-wristed hand. "Hi, I'm Lance and this is my boyfriend Jo" he said, rather like Julian Clairey.

"Oh shit, a gay golfer" I said to myself. Well there must be one out there somewhere, I thought.

"Yeah, hi there" I replied in my most butch accent.

I hit my drive off the first tee, a real beauty 300yds down the middle.

"Wow, aren't you a big boy?" said Lance all bulgy-eyed and jolly.

As Lance prepared to hit his shot I suddenly had a horrible thought, what if he can't play and he keeps hitting his golf balls into the trees and I have to help them look for a ball?

Now it's very poor golf etiquette if you're playing partner loses a ball and you don't help him look for it, but that would mean I would be in the trees with two homosexuals looking for a ball or two and very vulnerable.

"Fuck! please hit it straight" I whispered to myself.

As Lance skipped and lunged at his first shot, he somehow managed to hit it straight, about a hundred and fifty yards, but thank God it was in play.

"Good shot Lance" said Jo and applauded his effort. Lance jumped into his buggy and kissed Jo right on the lips.

"Thanks darling" he replied.

Oh Christ, this was going to be a long day, what had I done to deserve this? With the first hole out of the way, we drove the buggies around to the second.

There it was right in front of me, a potential disaster. Stroke index 1, 440 yards, par 4, thick trees each side and a very narrow fairway. Oh dear! Beads of sweat flowed from my forehead, this was a really demanding golf shot and I didn't really fancy it much myself. Taking an iron for safety, I managed to hit one about two hundreds yards, just short of the trees. Phew! That was lucky. Lance stepped up for his shot, took an almighty swing, skipped and jumped, closed his eyes, lifted his head and hit the ball. As it left the club I crossed my fingers and prayed.

"Please God, help me out here" I said.

Lance's ball set off like a banana and hooked violently left, deep into the trees.

"Oh shit!" I shouted.

Lance looked up, seemed delighted with his effort and bounced into the buggy with his boyfriend. As we approached the spot approximately where his ball had gone into the trees, the pair of them leapt out of the buggy and into the thick undergrowth. Now, I've seen the film" Deliverance" and I had a real dilemma here as I did not want to leave the safety of my golf buggy, but I should really, since it is good golf etiquette to help them look for the ball.

Oh what to do?

A sudden flash of inspiration! I backed my buggy up about fifteen feet and floored the accelerator, hurtling into the trees, creating a tunnel as I entered the woods. Branches and sticks everywhere, I was undeterred and drove round as if on safari looking for lions in the bush. Suddenly I spied Lance's ball lying on the ground in an open area.

"Lance, your balls' here mate" I shouted out to him.

Then I floored the buggy, penetrating back out through the trees and onto the course. As I looked around it was quite hilarious. There were two large gaping holes in the bushes, shaped perfectly to the size of the buggy.

Lance and Jo then appeared, looking disappointed that the ball had been found so quickly. Luckily no more disasters followed on that hole and as we headed for the next tee I was grateful to see that the course opened right up, the trees were fewer and far between and the only real hazards were lakes and bunkers.

On the 5th hole, Lance asked me what I did for a living. Hmmm! Right! Well, I couldn't say that I worked in the airlines or they would be clapping their hands, as ninety percent of male crew are gay.

"Yeah, um, I'm in real estate, sell houses in the UK" I said, lying through my teeth. "Oh really, me and Jo have a lovely house, you will have to come round one night" said Lance pouting his lips.

I choose not to reply to that one and was praying for the ninth hole and the club-house so that I could make my excuses and leg it. Telling a little white lie to the two of them that I had to go and meet my wife, I breathed a huge sigh of relief and headed back to the crew hotel to tell everybody of my hilarious mornings' adventures.

Sure enough, around the pool at the hotel the crews had taken up their usual positions. Manchester had their little spot away from everyone, sun beds positioned so they could get maximum rays and observe the Gatwick crew and make the usual bitchy comments about who was wearing what and hasn't she got a big bum etc. The two Gatwick crews kind of intermingled, paying little attention to no-one in particular. Making my way around the pool, I pulled up a sun bed and began to divulge my experiences of that morning's golf activities.

It was a beautiful day and the temperature was in the high nineties. After chatting and laughing for about half an hour it was time for lunch and as sixty crew members were all strewn around the pool, the back-drop was most appealing. In the bar area, a tannoy was installed to page guests to advise them that their food orders were ready. Knowing the bar staff quite well, they didn't mind me using the system to make a few announcements, much to the appreciation of the sun-bathing crews. Generally good fun banter about who was wearing the scariest swim pants, bits of juicy gossip, amusing anecdotes that went down well with the audience.

After my five minute cabaret and having finished lunch, I returned to my sun bed to catch the last few rays. As I positioned myself at the right angle, I caught a glimpse of a totally stunning girl, breathtaking actually. She was part of the crew on the other Gatwick flight and was chatting to someone I knew who used to go out with "The Housewives Favourite", Dougie Love; wow I had to go over and find out who she was. Feeling a little apprehensive (unusual for me) I approached the two girls and interrupted their conversation

"Hiya Claire, how are you?" I asked "The Housewives Favourite" ex-companion.

"Oh Hiya Gary, really well, I enjoyed your announcement earlier" she replied and both giggled simultaneously.

"Yes, just a bit of fun, who's your friend?" I asked inquisitively

"Oh yes, this is Debbie" said Claire. Our eyes met and I just knew there was something special about her. For the next twenty minutes the three of us sat there and laughed and chatted about airline stuff and I gave them a detailed account of my mornings' golfing activities, which Debbie found most entertaining. During the conversation it had come about that she was having real men trouble, well husband trouble actually, had split up and was really upset about the whole situation.

Although she was so beautiful looking she also had a wonderful personality and an easy going way about her, I had to get her telephone number somehow and find out a bit more about her. As it was nearly time for the wake-up call I had to think of a way of achieving this. I managed to get her surname at the end of our conversation and headed back to my room to check the

211

crew list that we received on arrival, sure enough there she was, second from the bottom, Debbie..........

Plucking up the courage, heart beating faster, I dialled her room.

"Hi Debbie, it's Gary, I was just talking to you by the pool. Um, I don't normally do this but I wonder if I could get your number and catch up with you back in the UK, maybe request a trip together or something?" I asked hopefully.

Sure enough Debbie was happy to give it to me and we exchanged numbers. I felt well happy with myself. I knew this was the person I'd been waiting for (even if she was married Plonker).On the flight home, I had difficulty not thinking about Debbie. My God, what a feeling! In order to distract myself I spent some time on the flight deck talking to the pilots.

Now pilots are a unique breed of people, they have massive responsibilities and at the end of the day, your life is in their hands. When you listen to them speaking over the PA system on board an aircraft, you want to hear the calm, collected voice of someone in control, invariably they all sound similar, a BBC type of upper-class accent. You will never hear a really dopey Brummie or a very strong Scouse accent coming out of the speakers as you sit there sipping your gin and tonic.

It is also very interesting to observe passengers if the pilot on the day happens to be female and starts talking over the PA system, suddenly seat-belts are fastened more tightly and people start to mumble nervously to each other. On one occasion I witnessed a most interesting conversation between a couple of upper-class passengers who were sitting near me when the lady Captain started to explain over the PA about the flight time etc.

"Christ it's a bloody woman pilot, "said one of the guys

"Yes shit! Women can't even reverse cars properly let alone fly a 747 Jumbo", replied the other.

Once pilots change out of their uniforms down-route and hit the hotel bar they do one of two things, either bore you to death with old flying stories or pretend they are 20 years younger and act like big kids. A number of pilots that I have encountered over the years were living two separate lives. Some of them had their little wives at home looking after the mock mansion in the country, two kids, dog etc, and then as soon as they were down-route, out of sight out of mind, a totally different person appeared, many of them had girlfriends in numerous destinations!! (Of course not all did, some were perfect gentlemen.)

However it was common place for affairs to spring up all over the place, typical of this was a situation I witnessed one winter flying into New York.

On the outbound flight I had been chatting to the crew in the cockpit about all sorts of subjects ranging from pensions to relationships and the First Officer James had commented to me about how much he loved his wife, how beautiful she was and how happy he was with his relationship, he produced photographs of his missus, the whole nine yards.

Not thinking anything else of it, the following morning I decided to take a stroll through Central Park and as it was winter a lovely covering of snow shimmered in the bright, sunny, crisp morning light, it was quite a beautiful setting.

As I looked around observing the surrounding skyscrapers in the distance, who should I see, non other than pilot James walking hand in hand with one of the junior cabin-crew.

As I turned to get a better look sheer panic fell over his face when he realised my presence, I smiled and shook my head in his direction. He immediately dropped the young lady's hand, laughed, joked and began to make quick small talk in an attempt to smokescreen my observations. After a couple of minutes an awkward silence fell over the conversation and I bid them farewell.

It's a small world sometimes!!!

The new breed of pilots that flew the Airbus A 340 were generally a good bunch of guys , on one occasion I remember being on the flight deck whilst landing at

Kai Tak airport in Hong Kong, there were about 10 people sat inside the cockpit, no seatbelts attached, nothing. (Probably would be unheard of today)

It was always good fun and a good wind-up to borrow the pilots cap and jacket during the flight and walk round the aircraft looking at the doors in a very concerned manner or tapping the fuselage then shaking your head in disbelief, the passengers' reactions were always priceless.

Wearing the Captains cap, jacket and headset, I would sit in the toilet holding a china dinner plate as a mock steering-wheel waiting for the stewardess to bring the kids for a flight deck visit. Since the stewardess was pre-warned she would knock on the door pretending it was the cockpit and I would sit there pretending to fly the plane. The kids who were expecting to see flashing lights and high-tech switches would look at you in total bemusement and shock.

I remember once a Captain was seeing one of the girls from the crew so he asked me if I could arrange for her to have the same break-time as him; I presumed he wanted to join the mile-high club.

Deciding this was too much of an opportunity to pass up, I advised the cabin-crew lady in question that her break-time was to commence at 12:15 in the pilot crew-rest area. However it wasn't normally supposed to start until 12:30 as the Flight Engineer was in there at that hour.

Sure enough the Captains girlfriend slipped out of her uniform and semi-naked entered the pitch black crew-rest area.

Suddenly a huge SCREAM was heard as the unsuspecting Flight Engineer couldn't believe his luck when a scantily clad hostess began to caress his body.

It was absolutely hilarious to watch as the young cabin crew member scuttled out of the bunks and into the toilet closely followed by the Flight Engineer, smiling like the proverbial Cheshire cat.

I don't think the Captain ever forgave me.

After airline crew have been away for a few days, one of their main priorities once all the passengers have disembarked is to check their mobile phones to see what messages they have received. Upon switching on mine the familiar bleep tone alerted me to my text messages. As I scrolled through them, Debbie's name leapt out at me. Heart beating faster I could hardly read her message.

"Really nice to meet you, I'm off to San Francisco on my next trip, see if you can get on it, Deb xx". You bet! I headed off to my parents place in Marlow for some relaxation and recuperation.

I spent the next few days talking and sending text messages to Debbie, also trying to get Virgin crewing to swap me onto the San Francisco flight that Debbie was on. They owed me a favour and John, the Crewing Manager, was looking into it for me. Luckily, the night before the trip John phoned to inform me that he had managed to sort it out and I was off to San Francisco.

"John, you're a star" I shouted down the phone.

"Yeah: No worries! enjoy your shag, whoever it is" he replied,

"No this one's special John, I swear" I responded.

"Yeah right, whatever, I hear that one hundreds of times" he said and hung up. I sent a text to Debbie to advise her that I'd sorted out San Francisco and she was delighted.

Although Debbie was married, she told me that it was all over and had been a disaster. She had married a policeman and the odd hours they both worked had made them drift apart, that she had been through a tough time and lost faith with the world a bit. The fact that she was still married did ring alarm bells inside me but she convinced me it was not a problem and was preparing to sort out the technical side of the marriage.

CHAPTER 30

THE PERFECT GENT!!??

VSO 23 to San Francisco was here. As luck would have it, on this flight I had three ex-rough and tumbles as part of the crew, just what you need when you're trying to build foundations and credibility with a potentially new girlfriend. As I was Purser and in charge of the working positions, I separated them off with military precision, so they would all be working in the opposite four corners of the plane. I, of course, would be working out of the same galley as Debbie and just hoped that the gossip would be limited and she wouldn't get upset on hearing about my prior casualties. All was going to plan until the services were more or less completed and it was time for the breaks. Nicky, one of my previous dates, came into the galley where Debbie and I were chatting. Oh dear!

"So Gazza, who are you shagging at the moment? I've sent you a load of messages but you've not been replying to them" said Nicky, pouting and hinting.

"Err, well, you know how it is, I've sort of got a new lady on board now, well hopefully, fingers crossed" I replied and looked at Debbie, who smiled and blushed.

"Gazza, you'll never settle down, anyway what have you got planned for us on this trip? Napa Valley or something similar?" asked Nicky as she observed Debbie.

"Not sure yet, I might have a quiet one" I answered, trying not to give too much away. Nicky left the galley and I could tell she was suspicious and wondering what I was up to.

I had seen Nicky for a bit when Lakey and I had split up, but she was as mad as a wasp and she found it difficult keeping her pants on. On a trip to Antigua she had a rough and tumble with Woody, so I had decided to keep her at arms length and ignore her text messages once I found out about the Woody saga. Airline life is so incestuous it's scary, someone has always shagged somebody who knows someone and gossip about it is rife. The problem is, if you do meet a person that you really like and they ask questions on different flights to others like "do you know anything about such and such?", everyone has an opinion and it's normally not too complimentary. The airline world is so easy to meet new people but sustaining a relationship within it is very, very difficult. A lot of crew adopt the policy: "I don't do crew as it always ends in tears".

As I tidied the galley, I caught Debbie looking at me inquisitively.

"So what's the story with Nicky?" she asked,

"Yeah, I had a bit of rough and tumble with her months ago, nothing in it. You know what airline life is like?" I replied, not too convincingly.

"Yeah I do, I know that you're a rascal Gary and a bit of a player, but I just want to have fun after the year I've had, that's why I like you, you're funny and you make me laugh" replied Debbie. I leant over and kissed her on the cheek. God she was so beautiful, looked good enough to eat.

I reassured her that whatever stories she would hear about me (and there would be many), not to pay any attention as the exaggeration factor was tenfold and just ask me and I would tell her the truth. With the flight out of the way we boarded the crew-bus and headed into the city of San Francisco. I sat with Debbie at the back holding hands out of sight of everyone. I mentioned to Nicky on the flight that I really liked Debbie but didn't elaborate as I knew she would tell the whole crew, gossip was her forte.

Passing Soldier Field American Football Stadium we dropped over the hill and down into San Francisco Bay. What a beautiful looking city, Bay Bridge, Alcatraz, the Golden Gate Bridge and skyscrapers all came into view as we nudged our way through the busy afternoon traffic.

That night most of the crew met in the crew-room for a couple of drinks and decide whatever everybody wanted to do on the trip. I normally organised a day out, but this time I wanted to spend some quality time with Debbie, so the crew would be left to their own devices; that meant one thing, shopping. Afterwards we headed down to a local Irish bar, Scruffy's for a couple of night-caps and a more intimate atmosphere. Debbie and I sat there drinking ice-cold Chardonnay, we chatted a bit about our families and what was going on with them. I told her a few mad stories about my life and we laughed and chinked glasses. I had only just met her but it felt like we had known each other for years, the chemistry was perfect and I felt totally happy and comfortable. We spent the night back at my room, no sex, just kissing and cuddling, which was magic. I wanted to be the perfect gent and not rush straight into it.

The following morning I had organised a special day out for myself and Debbie to enjoy. We were off to Socalito, a tiny harbour village situated a few miles from San Francisco. We caught the cable-car tram down to Fisherman's Wharf and hired a couple of bikes. From there it was over the Golden Gate Bridge, stopping for a few minutes to gaze at the spectacular view, then continued our journey along the quaint, winding roads and down into Socalito itself.

It was such a beautiful place with a wonderfully safe ambiance about it. We locked up the bikes and took a stroll along the seafront, gazing into shop windows selling antiques and local souvenirs. I knew an excellent restaurant at the end of the village that looked right across the bay of San Francisco. It was time for lunch and there wasn't a better place to be.

Here I was, sitting with the woman of my dreams, drinking a glass of wine, looking across the bay of San Francisco and not a cloud in the sky. I was the happiest man in the world. We continued our conversations from the previous night over the next couple of hours and a few bottles of wine; I think we covered every subject on the planet. What a super day! As the sun was dropping off it was time to head back. We caught the ferry from Socalito to Fisherman's Wharf, admiring the views that were a sight to behold.

Back on dry land I kissed Debbie and she thanked me for a lovely day.

"No problem, it was my pleasure" I said lovingly.

"What do you fancy doing now" I continued,

"I think we should go to my room and have a lie down" she replied with glinting eyes. Excellent news!

A taxi back to the hotel and it was time for a moment I would not forget for the rest of my life. Debbie had such a fantastic body, was passionate, loving and when you care about someone those feelings are so much more enriched. As we lay there holding each other, I felt like the luckiest man in the world. After a couple more hours of reposing, room-service delivered and consumed, I had a fantastic proposition for Debbie.

"Why don't we book a limo tonight and get it to drive around San Francisco, taking in all the sights, whilst drinking champagne and whatever else we might want to do" I suggested

"Yeah that's a brilliant idea" replied Debbie excitedly. After a quick shower and change of clothes, we headed off down to reception. I spoke to the Concierge about what we wanted, limo, champagne etc, and fifteen minutes later, our black, stretch-limo pulled up in front of the hotel. Its tinted windows and stretched-out interior were perfect for our trip around the city. I advised the driver of the route we wanted to take, not to disturb us and to keep the screen that divided the front from the back, up and closed at all times for obvious reasons. We eased into the luxury leather seats and headed off into the night as romantic, chill-out music eased from the speakers and, with champagne on ice, everything seemed perfect.

We arrived at Lombard Street, the famous, winding road seen in many films. I took Debbie's hands and we began to kiss passionately. She was wearing a tiny, black skirt and top with nothing underneath, this was amazing, driving around San Francisco at night in a limo, making love to a beautiful woman. Going across the Golden Gate Bridge I had Debbie on top, totally naked, moaning and grinding away. It was a great feeling knowing that the tinted windows on the limo were protecting our activities from any prying eyes. What a rush and a blinding experience that capped the most perfect day.

The following morning after breakfast in bed and (breakfast), it was time for the usual pre-flight check-out procedures. This normally involved shopping at the airline crews' favourite stores, like Banana Republic, Macy's, The Gap and Marcus Neumann. Walking around Macy's, I spotted a very nice Ralph Lauren bag that I was sure Debbie would like. Out of sight I purchased it to give her on the flight home. After such a great trip and the relationship with Debbie moving to the next level or even further, I was in a particularly good mood.

The voyage back was hassle-free and just before the crew breaks began, I handed Debbie her little present that I had bought for her and wrapped up, telling her to open it when no one was looking. She disappeared off to the toilet and I organised the galley with orange and water set-ups that would keep the passengers hydrated on the flight back to the UK. Debbie returned to the galley, kissed me on the cheek and thanked me for the bag and the brilliant trip she'd just had.

MADE LOVE ON OUR CREW REST BREAK TOGETHER. HAPPY DAYS!

Back in the UK and it was time for a few days off. Debbie was heading to her home town of Norwich and I was off to Newcastle. Over the next couple of days we spent a fortune on phone calls and text messages. She invited me down to meet her family, a nerve racking experience, but I was happy to do so.

(My God, I think I might be in love). That was it! For the next couple of months we were inseparable, swapping onto each others flights, days off together, flying all over the world, enjoying a millionaires champagne lifestyle on lemonade money. The only bad news I had in that time was a letter from Virgin to say that my new Line Manager was, of all people, "The Crow". Now that was a disaster and would prove pivotal for my career.

The Crow had been promoted and would be spending more time on the ground in the cabin-crew main office and less time in the air which was a good thing. However, once or twice a month she would be doing flight assessments to make sure all was in order and would be assessing me in the coming few months. Oh what joy! Apart from that and Debbie's husband turning up at the house with a bouquet of flowers to apologise for his behaviour, breaking into tears and collapsing in the garden punching the ground hysterically, life had never been better.

CHAPTER 31

THE WRONG DECISION

A group of us, including Debbie, the Muskrat and a couple of the Venga Boys had requested a five night Cape Town trip together to enjoy the sights and sounds of this wonderful part of the world. When the rosters came out, to my horror I had not been given the trip. My bid had been intercepted by The Crow and she had put me on a three night flight to Narita, Japan and would be assessing me.

My decision on what I was going to do about this problem would be the most important pivotal moment of my life so far.

After speaking to a few of my close work associates, I made the decision to phone in sick for my flight to Japan with The Crow and go off to Cape Town with Debbie and all my friends on a staff concession ticket. Loads of people phoned in sick and disappeared all over the world, and as I had a spare staff ticket I had not yet used for the year I decided to go for it. As I had been employed with the company a fair few years I had a really good boarding priority on the standby system for staff travel. Everyone was trying to get companions out for this trip so it was a little bit competitive to see who would get on and who wouldn't. In the end most of the staff standbys made it although most were allocated seats down the back in economy, whilst Muskrat and I were fully reclined, drinking champagne served by our girlfriends. Happy days!

The journey to Cape Town was great; staying at the beautiful Collin Hotel in the centre of Cape Town was the perfect location to explore all the sites. On this trip we did everything from absailing down table-top mountain to wine tasting, cricket on the beach and a visit to Cape Horn, the very tip of South Africa where the Atlantic meets the Pacific Ocean, a "must see" in your life. I was so happy with Debbie and we were becoming very close. After the break it was time to head home. Now using staff travel is a very cost effective way of travelling around the world, but the stress factor of "Am I getting on or not?' can take the shine off it sometimes.

With at least forty staff passengers trying to get home from Cape Town to Heathrow the pressure was on and everybody was on edge, hoping.

Luckily for me I had the highest priority on the standby list, my name was called out first and I was allocated the last seat in upper-class, much to the annoyance of Jo, a staff member from crewing who was bitterly disappointed that I had been given the last seat in "J" class and she would have to settle for premium economy. In the end most of the standby got on and we were back in the UK.

Once home it was off to Norwich to prepare for Christmas and sort out the New Year's party. Debbie and I were off to LAX skiing, we were also taking her Dad and a couple of friends and were really looking forward to it. Unbeknown to me, Jo from crewing, who had been in Cape Town and hadn't got the upper-class seat she was expecting, had checked my roster on her computer when returning to work and realised I shouldn't have been on the flight as I was signed off sick; she then passed this information onto The Crow.

The Crow being the busybody bitch from hell that she is, decided to make detailed enquires about where I had been and why I had phoned in sick and not gone to Japan with her. While doing some Christmas shopping in Norwich, she phoned me on my mobile to ask me to come to the office for a little chat. I knew she had found out about my trip, but as loads of people had done the same thing before, I thought I was going to get a slap on the wrist and that was it. When I arrived at the cabin-crew office in Horley, Surrey, I made my way to the Line Managers' office for a 'casual chat', as The Crow had put it when she called me.

CHAPTER 32

THE NOT SO CASUAL CHAT

When I arrived, I knew I had been well and truly stitched up. Four Line Managers were waiting there, which in the history of the airline was unheard of, especially during casual, informal chats of this nature. I was being set up and hung out to dry. As The Crow began her interrogation, not a chat at all, she scowled and glared at me, smirking within and milking this moment for all its worth, she had got me by the bollocks and she knew it. With no official union to back me up, something I had been canvassing for years much to the disgust of the management, I was treading on very thin ice. I listened to the detailed account of her investigation that had been carefully put together and must have taken days. She had listed times, places, the lot and had gone into meticulous detail and had conned me into thinking that I was coming in for a casual chat, what a vindictive bitch. Sitting silently in the room, listening to The Crow's evidence, I knew I had made a mistake and shouldn't have gone to Cape Town but I was a fun loving person, had fallen in love and probably wasn't thinking straight and hadn't realised the consequences of my actions. I loved doing the job I cared about people and enjoyed life.

Here I was, listening to this person, who all the crews despised, who hated life, men and pretty, young girls, would reduce people to tears every time she flew, caused people to resign from the airline and now she had the power to get rid of me and was going to seize the opportunity.

I kept silent throughout the entire interview and just stared into her dark eyes that were empty of emotion, knowing that one day everybody would find out what a calculating, evil bitch, she was. Pure nasty!

I had been flying for seven years, made lots of close friends, had wonderful experiences and stories to tell and now due to one person's personal desire, because I was not like her and she was "just doing her job" as she put it, I would be out of the job I loved.

They didn't say I would be sacked at that point, only advised me that a full disciplinary hearing would take place the following week, but I knew my days were numbered. Feeling like I had been crushed by a steamroller I left the building and called Debbie. She was really upset for me and tried to console my devastated mind, telling me that they wouldn't sack me that they were just trying to make a point and frighten me;

I had a feeling they were going to make an example of me. Because I was such a high profile figure within the airline and quite outspoken, I suspected by sacking me, it would send out a very clear message: no union, no rights, we have the power and not individual cabin-crew members.

At the time there was also an epidemic of people travelling on staff concessions who were sick etc. I had one more trip to do before the disciplinary, Newark New York.

The flight to Newark (New York) was so sad knowing that I was on my way, I was shell-shocked and walking around like a zombie. I confided to the In-flight Supervisor, Maurice, about what was going down and he was great, taking on all my duties as well as his own as I just couldn't think straight.

I knew I had fucked up but for God's sake, I hadn't killed anyone, hadn't stolen anything, punched or abused anyone. All I had done was fall in love and make a daft decision.

Walking around New York on that freezing cold December morning, I had a tear in my eye. As I looked up at the Empire State Building and the Twin Towers, little did I know that less than nine months later the

Twin Towers would have disappeared as well! At the end of that flight I made an announcement to all the crew that this would be my last one. Everyone was genuinely gutted as they could see how upset and emotional I was. If only by some miracle they decided to give me a final written warning, or six month demotion or loss of travel concessions for a year, but not take somebody's livelihood away from them. I hadn't told my parents yet about my disciplinary as I didn't want to worry them unduly, after all I still had a one percent chance of keeping my job.

The day of the disciplinary, the 11th December 2001, arrived. As I entered the Line Manager's open plan office you could cut the atmosphere with a knife. The Pink Mafia representation and an official from the Human Resources department were openly chatting to Colin Schnell, president of the Pink Mafia. As I walked towards them they stopped chatting and dispersed, heads down, heading into their separate offices.

Colin Schnell was the Cabin Crew General Manager and a double of the lead singer of the Petshop Boys in everyway.

I had little to do with him over the years, but there was little love lost between us, he knew all about me and my opinions in life. As soon as I saw him chatting to the two people doing my disciplinary I knew my one percent chance had just evaporated. This was a stitch-up and it had just been confirmed.

As I approached the interview room door I saw The Crow. She sat there with a smug grin on her ugly face, wallowing in my obvious discomfort that she had instigated. She knew that in half an hour I was history. Yeah okay, stitch someone up if you're that way inclined but don't sit there in front of the person and deliberately stoke up their emotions. The suffering was bad enough and to milk it to that degree made my blood boil. At that point I wish now that I had gone over and banged her head against the concrete pillow by her desk.

Sure enough the outcome was a foregone conclusion and the words: "we have decided in this case you should be dismissed" that came across to me in slow motion, will live for with me forever (a bullet to the head). I was in obvious shock even though I had pretty much guessed the outcome before the actual hearing; I was just hoping they would cut me a bit of slack. N.F.W! I was the wrong colour, the wrong gender and I was out.

As I left the building it was the lowest point in my life, a real sledgehammer blow, just as everything was going so well. The following week I had been rostered on a ski trip to LAX with Debbie and were taking a couple of friends, all that was now cancelled. What a nightmare! I phoned all my good friends in the airline who were waiting anxiously for the news and the verdict.

On informing them one by one, they were all gutted and upset, arguing that the punishment was too harsh and that I should appeal the decision. Finally I called Debbie, who was on her way to New York, who screeched in horror then cried and sobbed uncontrollably. This set me off. God what a mess! So unnecessary! To wreck someone's life and jeopardise their livelihood was appalling and probably just a big game to them. My worst thought was to have to go and explain everything to my parents as they hadn't a clue what was happening to me and would be totally devastated. What a thing to have to do.

On leaving the offices in Horley I headed to Philo Beddo's place in Crawley, where a couple of my good friends were waiting. On route I passed The Ranch, where so many brilliant things had occurred and it made me feel so sad. The lads were cool and tried to lift my spirits but I was an empty shell and in pure shock.

The journey back to Marlow and my parent's house was awful, how was I going to tell them what had happened? It was something I was really dreading. I will never forget my Mum's little face as I told them the details of what had happened during the previous twelve hours. Many, many tears were shed.

When Debbie returned from JFK there was so much to sort out. My head was in such a total spin and with Christmas just around the corner, what timing for this to happen. I didn't know what I was going to do. I had two mortgages to sort out, debts and all the usual money commitments. So many pressures building up on top of what had happened, my world was in a downward spiral and spinning out of control. If I wasn't careful now I would lose everything. I had to try and get a foothold somewhere, I had promised to try and help Debbie with her financial situation, and sort things out.

Luckily family and friends were stepping in to help me financially but I didn't really know where I should be. The beauty of flying is that it didn't matter really where in the UK you lived, you were totally flexible and only had to be in the London area (Gatwick or Heathrow) once a week for your flight. Now with my house in Newcastle, parents in Marlow a girlfriend in Norwich and out of a job, something had to give.

Debbie's husband had discovered my situation and stepped in, offering Debbie the works; let's buy a house together, I'm all sorted, blah, blah, fucking blah, Gazza is shafted and no use to you anymore etc; one can only imagine the spin doctoring that occurred. It was true though, I needed to snap out of my situation but that was easier said than done. I was wounded and rolling fast down a steep hill. It's an awful feeling when you're no longer in control of your destiny.

Eventually, St.Valentines day arrived; Debbie and I decided to have a sabbatical separation to see in which direction things were heading. The bottom line was Debbie had financial difficulties. I had lost my job and couldn't afford now to pay for the lifestyle I had created for myself. Her husband had offered a lifeline of security and Debbie was going to go for it (how gutted was I). I had lost the job I adored, lost the girl I loved and was about to lose the house for which I had worked so damned hard and all because of my mistake and a busybody Crow (revenge is sweet). Life can be so cruel sometimes!

CHAPTER 33

LIFE IS REALITY

Over the coming weeks, with events and circumstances in my life falling apart before my eyes I was falling into a terminal depression that I couldn't stop. At that time my parents and very close friends were deeply concerned for my well being and had seen a larger than life character, that loved life, made people laugh and smile and be happy, reduced to a solemn, distant, deeply depressed person they hardly recognised (how tragic!).

At the beginning of March a trip that had been organised six months earlier to the ski resort of St Anton was upon us, four days of fun and laughs in the mountains. I really didn't want to go but my parents and close friends were adamant, they thought it would be a good thing and would help me on the road to recovery. After landing at Geneva airport, the group of us took the three hour train journey to the St Anton ski resort in the Austrian Alps. It was a really beautiful place and the most tranquil, relaxed resort I had ever seen. A fairytale, winter-wonderland village, fantastic chalets and hotels, nestled amongst some beautiful mountain valleys. I should have been buzzing about the place, yet I felt sad and alone (how strange, here I was in one of the most beautiful places in the world, yet felt so sad and distracted).

I had been skiing for about fifteen years so was very confident and could ski to an advanced level. People have told me that when you ski it reflects your mood. This is so true! For three days I skied right on the edge, taking crazy risks, going in and out of narrow, tree-lined, off-piste ski areas without regard for safety and pushing myself to the limits of sanity. I think I was almost goading the Ski-Gods to decide on my fate in life!

The après skis for those four days was a total blur, a countless number of beers, wine, Sambucca shots and Glühwein in various bars and taverns. It all seemed to be a big haze. The last ski-day had arrived and the weather was grey and very cold, a hard frost from the previous night had firmed up all the slopes and skiing was hazardous, even for the most accomplished experts. Without a care in the world I skied even more aggressively, almost reaching crazy limits. Muskrat stopped me on the way up in a chairlift and told me to calm down. He had been observing me over the last couple of days and was deeply concerned. I reassured him I was fine and not to worry. After a few drinks for lunch and before it was time for the last ski session of the trip, I was relaxing on the terrace, soaking up the brilliant sunshine and daydreaming.

I had taken the cable-car to the very top to start the very demanding black run descent downhill. Goggles fixed into place, I pushed off and headed down the mountain, my mind was racing out of control, I felt like a man on speed running down a narrow alley searching for an exit. Why was this happening? I had skied down this mountain a number of times and was pushing myself to beat my fastest time. I remembered seeing what I thought was a shortcut and try to shave a few precious seconds off my previous best effort.

As I thundered down the mountain, taking more and more risks, increasing my speed, I was skiing beyond my limits and the edges of my skis searched frantically for a grip as I turned into what I had determined to be the shortcut.

In front of me, red and white plastic tape blocked my path with the warning sign: "*Achtung*: Ski-Fahren verboten." imprinted on my eyes. But it was too late. I just couldn't stop and snapped through the tape like an Olympic champion. It wasn't a shortcut at all, but a severe cliff drop! Silently, I was flying, tumbling freely through the ice-cold air".

A tap on my shoulder brought me back to reality. I opened my eyes. My parents and friends were looking at me in a strange way. I wasn't dead as I had imagined. I was well and truly alive. I had not fallen into the abyss of my dreams, but my life was sure as hell heading that way.

This was my wake-up call and I had to do something very fast to prevent that dream becoming reality.

THE END

EPILOGUE

It is very interesting how events can alter the course of your life. After leaving Austria I decided to get a firm grip on my life and get it back on track. I now live on the island of Tenerife for most of the year, where I moved to five years ago and set myself up in business. I am now semi-retired after selling that business. This gave me the time to write the book as well as enjoy the fruits of life and improve my dodgy golf handicap at the same time.

Tenerife is a most unique place to live. It has a wonderful year round temperature, fascinating characters and hidden beauty. I think at some point in the near future I will write about my experiences on how to survive and succeed on this mad island they call Tenerife, until that time remember this ....

"IF YOUR NOT LIVING LIFE ON THE EDGE, YOUR TAKING UP TOO MUCH ROOM "

HASTA LA VISTA!!!!

About the Author

Having recently sold my business in Tenerife, I have had time to sit back, reflect on my life and decided to put pen to paper. This book is all about my real life experiences with Virgin Airlines, dating from 1994 through to 2001.

This is a true down to earth but, at the same time humorous account of what went on behind the scenes during my term of employment as seen through my own eyes.

Printed in the United Kingdom by
Lightning Source UK Ltd., Milton Keynes
142212UK00001BA/21/A